"The principles and profound qu[...]
pages have the power to radically [...]
for how my friend Ben Pilgreen h[...]
but also lived this message. In ma[...]
out of me things I didn't know were there. His curiosity for life
and care for others come through in the pages of this book. I
can't wait to see what comes out of many more people getting
this message."

Andy Wood, lead pastor of Saddleback Church

"At last! A simple book that provides a meaningful framework
on life's biggest questions of who, why, what, and where. I love
the way that Ben has put together something that is elegantly
simple and applicable on the other side of the theological com-
plexity. I'm a big fan of him and this book!"

Henry Kaestner, cofounder of Bandwidth and
Faith Driven Entrepreneur

"There never has been and never will be anyone like you. That
isn't a testament to you. It's a testament to the God who created
you. This book will help you discover who and whose you are.
And Ben will help you bring it out!"

Mark Batterson, *New York Times* bestselling author of
The Circle Maker; lead pastor of National Community Church

"This works. There's no greater endorsement I can give. Having spent countless hours with high-impact people in various
cultures, I've become repulsed by generic platitudes that feel
better than they function. The chapters about selecting and
leveraging a wisdom table alone are worth the book's weight in
gold. Ben provides a practical road map to live the exceptional
life you were meant to live, how exhilarating it will be, and why
the world will be better if you do."

Joseph King Barkley, Novus Global executive coach;
president of the Meta Performance™ Institute

"Some things have an exponential ability to release power,
and Ben has captured this in his book. By taking seriously the
differences that lie in each of us and finding ways not to be

intimidated or frustrated by them, but rather to unleash them, we have the ability to make our organizations and our lives move toward the extraordinary we have always hoped for."

Nancy Ortberg, CEO, Transforming the Bay with Christ

"One of the limiting beliefs that holds us back is that we must achieve our goals alone. If you desire to live a life of purpose but feel dissatisfied with your current trajectory, *Bring It Out* can help you harness the collective wisdom of a trusted advisory group, referred to as the wisdom table. Ben not only unveils the significance of this approach but also guides you through the process of what, why, and how to utilize this invaluable resource to launch you closer to achieving your life's goals."

Jasmine Lawrence, founder of EDEN BodyWorks

"In a Silicon Valley ecosystem filled with business gurus patting themselves on the back and pontificating about 'making the world a better place,' Ben has been quietly uploading (or incepting, in some cases) wisdom into the brains of entrepreneurs, investors, and change-makers here in Silicon Valley to great effect. *Bring It Out* is chock-full of practical wisdom learned over decades that can be applied to your life today so you can discover the unique and significant giftedness God has put inside of you that he wants to bring out of you. 'Making the world a better place' is vague and vulnerable to narcissists and sociopaths. I prefer 'participating faithfully in God's plan for creation.' *Bring It Out* can help you get there."

Trae Stephens, partner, Founders Fund; cofounder, Anduril

"Ben has created an elegant thought construct to discover and activate the best version of yourself. The key principles are simultaneously powerful guidelines for understanding your greater purpose and a practical playbook for navigating everyday life."

Reed Dickens, founder and CEO of LA GOLF

"You have an assignment, and it's unique to you. The challenge for most of us is that finding this assignment is similar to looking for buried treasure with a confusing map. My friend Ben Pilgreen has been guiding people to finding their assignment for years now, and thanks to his book he's now helping you. *Bring It Out* will help you, but it will also help the rest of us. We need you to bring out your unique assignment. You'll help us get better when you do."

Jeff Henderson, author of *What to Do Next*

"Whether you're young or old, discovering your purpose is paramount. And Ben provides a powerful and practical road map for not only discovering your purpose but truly living it out."

Brad Lomenick, former president of Catalyst;
author of *The Catalyst Leader* and *H3 Leadership*

"*Bring It Out* is a decade's worth of teaching in a day's worth of reading. Part personal vulnerability, part encouragement, part inspiration, part exhortation, Ben does in this book what he does best from the stage—packaging the truths of life into applicable nuggets of wisdom to help us all live more into the reality of who we are."

Ben Chelf, cofounder and CEO of Sol

"When leaders of Silicon Valley seek wise counsel, they call on Ben Pilgreen. In *Bring It Out*, you'll learn how God designed you for greatness—and how to step into his vision for your life. Ben generously shares the principles and perspectives that have enabled him to start up a thriving church against all odds and influence many people to realize their full God-given potential. Get ready to be inspired, challenged, and equipped!"

Denise Lee Yohn, bestselling author of
What Great Brands Do and *FUSION*

BRING
IT
OUT

BRING
IT
OUT

How to Cultivate the
Unique Gifts and Assignments
You've Been Given

BEN PILGREEN

Revell

a division of Baker Publishing Group
Grand Rapids, Michigan

Published by Revell
a division of Baker Publishing Group
Grand Rapids, Michigan
RevellBooks.com

Printed in the United States of America

Library of Congress Cataloging-in-Publication Data
Names: Pilgreen, Ben, 1977– author.
Title: Bring it out : how to cultivate the unique gifts and assignments you've been given / Ben Pilgreen.
Description: Grand Rapids, Michigan : Revell, a division of Baker Publishing Group, [2024] | Includes bibliographical references.
Identifiers: LCCN 2023038491 | ISBN 9780800745776 (paper) | ISBN 9780800745929 (casebound) | ISBN 9781493445592 (ebook)
Subjects: LCSH: Gifts—Religious aspects—Christianity.
Classification: LCC BR115.G54 P55 2024 | DDC 234/.13—dc23/eng/20240126
LC record available at https://lccn.loc.gov/2023038491

Cover design by Terry Rohrbach, Fort Studio

Baker Publishing Group publications use paper produced from sustainable forestry practices and postconsumer waste whenever possible.

24 25 26 27 28 29 30   7 6 5 4 3 2 1

For Shauna. You bring out the best in me.

Contents

Section Four What Will Help You?

Foreword

The California Bay Area is one of the least churched regions of our nation. Of the nearly eight million people in the area's eleven counties (including Santa Cruz and Monterey), close to five million are unchurched or have no religious affiliation whatsoever. Additionally, many existing churches live a siloed and isolated existence. Why would anyone want to come here to start a church? Who would want to plant a church here?

The New Testament shows us the gospel coming into the most challenging, hardest soil of ancient times. Why? Because that's where the need was the greatest. "The seed falling on good soil refers to someone who hears the word and understands it. This is the one who produces a crop, yielding a hundred, sixty or thirty times what was sown" (Matt. 13:23).

Each of us has been given a significant calling. I'm called to lead a turnaround of the very company that put the silicon in Silicon Valley. Ben Pilgreen was called to come to San Francisco—one of the most challenging cities in the Bay Area, our nation, and the world—and plant a growing church. God has uniquely skilled and prepared each of us for these assignments. The twists, turns, and failures of life were not distractions but preparations and step-ups for each of us into the next leg of the journey that God prepared for us.

I'm so encouraged and proud to know that Ben heeded the call. In this book, he pulls from that and provides valuable thoughts on how each of us can best be seeing, preparing for, and navigating the challenges of that journey. Who are the members seated at your wisdom table? Is it filled with those who can help you see the wisdom of the moment and how it applies to your life?

As a public company CEO, I carefully manage and work with my board of directors to harness and benefit from the many decades of wisdom they bring to me and the board. Who is the board of directors for your most important asset—the rest of your life? Have you carefully selected those you want at that table? Do you regularly seek their counsel?

Of course, there will be more than a few challenges and distractions on the way. Ben gives some valuable tools and thoughts for how to navigate some of the hard things and be prepared to change from the comfortable to the direction and roles we are being called to. God does his best work in the midst of our discomfort.

God has called Ben and me to be church and workplace ministers in this magical, wonderful, and very spiritually tough soil of Silicon Valley. I'm sure you'll find Ben's learnings to be moving to your life. If they work here in Silicon Valley, they'll likely work wherever in the world you might be as well.

Pat Gelsinger
CEO, Intel; founder and chair,
Transforming Bay with Christ

Introduction

It's in You for a Reason

There has never been another human just like you. There never will be another human just like you. This means your Creator has put things in you he hasn't put in anyone else, at least not with the same specification. It's so easy to feel like there's nothing special or significant about who you are or what you can bring to the world. In fact, it's become way too common for many of us to apologize for who we are or to feel bad about what we can't do.

I'm sitting here in San Francisco, the city that has been my home since 2010. This is the last place I ever thought I would call home. And starting a thriving church in downtown San Francisco is the last thing I ever thought I'd do. It's a wonder this church even exists and an even bigger miracle I got to play a part in bringing it into reality. I smile as I think about how a guy like me ended up in a city like San Francisco. What has become the new normal for me, my family, and an entire faith community is far beyond what I ever could have imagined. I would love to take you on a journey of how this happened, but not just so I can tell you my story. My hope in writing this book is to show you what can be possible in your life. I have a deep belief I live by, and it's also why I wrote this book:

Whatever God put in you, he wants to bring out of you.

I'm not simply talking about starting a church or a business or becoming famous or doing something the world would think is amazing. What I'm referring to is you getting in on whatever God may have for you in this life. It could be losing weight or losing your short temper. It could be running a marathon or running an organization in your community. It could be enjoying a healthy marriage or enjoying a global adventure. It could be making a difference in your neighborhood or raising kids who will change the world.

We all know what it's like to have dreams. Or maybe the more accurate way to say it is, we at least know what it's like to have *had* dreams. There was a point in all our lives when we knew where we wanted to end up, but relatively few of us arrived at our preferred destination.

Have you ever had a moment or season in your life that left you saying, "This wasn't the dream"? The dream was to have an amazing marriage; you weren't supposed to be divorced. The dream was that you would be an executive by now; you weren't planning on being stuck in your career. The dream was that your new company would get off the ground, except it never really took off. The dream you had for your life didn't include anxiety and depression, yet these emotions have become daily companions for you.

We don't have a desire problem. Most of us even started down the right path. But at some point, for a variety of reasons, we lost our way. Perhaps someone else or a group of people destroyed what could have been in our lives. Maybe we chose the wrong thing to pursue. The problem could have been that we surrounded ourselves with the wrong people. Or we found ourselves paralyzed with fears we simply could not overcome. It could even be we were really clear on the ultimate goal, but we couldn't figure out the steps needed to get there. Maybe we underestimated the cost it would take for our dream to come true. Or we got off to a great start, but we weren't able to sustain it over the long haul.

Before you push away whatever God put in your heart, I would love to come alongside you to share stories and principles that will provide a path to your preferred future. Don't worry, I'm not going to promise you anything is possible in your life. However, I think there's a good chance way more is possible than what you're experiencing right now. And the framework I'm going to give you won't just help you in the "major" areas of your life. These ideas have also helped me to become a morning person, to give thirty-minute talks without using notes, to lead a family of six who is thriving in an urban environment, to get back down to my high school weight, and much more. I still get stuck at times, but I keep returning to these principles. And it starts with this one:

Whatever God put in me, he wants to bring out of me.

Throughout this book, I want to show you the kinds of things that will help you fulfill your purpose. I also want to warn you about the kinds of things that will keep you from seeing your vision become reality. What if you could step into a life full of meaning and purpose? Can you picture yourself being deeply fulfilled while also making an impact on the lives of others? What if there's a clear path between where you are today and where you want to be one day? I not only think this is possible; I genuinely believe this is the life you were meant for.

What Has God Put within You?

*The only person you can take into any environment
is the person you have become.*

1

Who Matters Most

"What am I supposed to do with my life?" This is a great question. It's one I have asked throughout my lifetime, and I get asked some version of it on a regular basis. When most people ask this question, here's what they mean: "What am I meant to do?" And even more specific than that, they usually mean, "What work am I called to do?"

I think what we do really matters, and you'll soon be reading an entire chapter on this idea. In fact, so much of this book is about bringing out the work that God put you on earth to produce. But before we get to what you are supposed to do, there's something even more fundamental you can nail down. Here's the formula I want you to embed in your heart and mind:

Who > Why > How > What

Who you become matters more than what you do. Why you do what you do matters more than what you do. How you do what you do matters more than what you do. And what you do still really matters.

If you become the right kind of person, it is likely you'll do the right thing. If you don't become the right kind of person, will it even matter what you do?

It is so easy to let who we have been keep us from becoming who we can be. We all have things in our past we are less than proud of. While it's okay to regret who we were in previous seasons of our lives, we cannot stay consumed with that. Imagine if the apostle Paul had been unable to get over his past. He had quite the past, didn't he? He gave his time and energy to arresting Christians in the first century and approving of their murders. What if this had paralyzed him from carrying out God's purpose for his life? I'm guessing he wouldn't have started so many churches or written around half of the New Testament. How did he let go of his past so he could step into the future? He revealed part of his secret when he shared these words: "forgetting what is behind and straining toward what is ahead" (Phil. 3:13).

You cannot move forward when you are fixated on what's behind you.

The world is going to tell you to work on your skills, grow your competencies, become more productive . . . and I'm all for those things. But when was the last time someone out there encouraged you to work on your character, the essence of who you are? Dallas Willard said, "The most important thing in your life is not what you do; it's who you become."[1]

It really matters who you are becoming. Whoever you are becoming—this is the person you bring to your parenting. This is the human who goes with you into your dating relationship. This is the man or woman who is part of your church community. This is the only person you can actually bring to work with you every day. And this is the human being who will step into eternity with you one day.

In our increasingly individualistic world, we are told we can be whoever we want to be. That sounds inspirational on the surface, but it's simply not true. We cannot be whoever we want to be, but we can be whoever God wants us to be. When it comes to who we are and who we will become, God has a part and we have a part. Often the problem for us is we are asking God to play our part while we try to step in and play the part reserved for him. Let me offer you some encouragement and a challenge. God is always going to play his part in who we become. He's not holding out on us. Be encouraged by that. There are so many times when he gives us a promise about who we can become. The challenge, however, is for us to be willing to play our part in the process.

As you read through the life of Jesus, you will discover he was constantly giving the disciples their part: "Follow me" (Matt. 4:19). He used that imperative when he called Levi the tax collector. Those are the words he used when restoring Peter after his denial of Jesus. He didn't tell these people they had to figure it all out on their own. He just told them to follow him.

If you're like me, there are days when you wonder if you will ever become the person God intends for you to be. When I find myself thinking this way, I'm so comforted by these words from Philippians 1:6: "Being confident of this, that he who began a good work in you will carry it on to completion until the day of Christ Jesus." With this in mind, here is an equation that's been helpful for me as I seek to become who God wants me to be.

Direction > Destination

Your direction is more important than your destination. This is something I try to remember in my parenting, and it helps me understand how God sees us. With my own kids, I need to remember I'm developing them on a daily basis rather than giving them a final grade every single day. I think God is the same with us. He isn't fixated on who we are today, but he is very interested in who we are becoming. And here's even better news—God sees us not only as we are but as we will be someday. As Ken Costa says, "Jesus knows who we are. But he also knows who we are becoming. He has a vested interest in seeing us flourish in the future."[2]

We think a lot about career trajectory. We don't typically give as much time to our character trajectory. When we see gaps in our professional lives, we find ways to fill those so we can get promoted or get a raise. But what if we started addressing our character gaps in the same way? When you think about the gap between who you are today and who you long to be, what would fill that gap? Look at the fruit of the Spirit (Gal. 5:22–23). It could be you need more love, joy, peace, patience, kindness, goodness, faithfulness, gentleness, or self-control.

> **As you consider your current character trajectory, do you like where you're headed? If not, what adjustments would help you to align your character with the person you want to be in the future?**

I'm making a few assumptions about you. I'm guessing you want to become the person God created you to be. I bet there are some areas of your character you would love to grow in. I even believe you want to change some things about yourself, but you aren't sure you'll be able to see this happen in your lifetime.

There are things we want to bring out in our lives, but we keep focusing on the results, often without much luck. What if, to get the outcomes we want, we don't spend a ton of time focusing on those outcomes?

I believe God gives us the secret to how we can see character growth in our lives. Listen in on some of the greatest wisdom ever shared: "Above all else, guard your heart, for everything you do flows from it" (Prov. 4:23). This is a strong word to us. "Above all else"—we should always pay attention to anything that follows this phrase. It's as if Solomon, who wrote Proverbs 4, is saying, "More than anything else, do this." Why is he so emphatic on making sure you guard your heart? Because everything flows from it. Whatever gets into your heart is going to be carried out in your life.

In the Bible, the heart means the center of you—your emotions, your desires, what is core to who you are. If everything flows out of the heart, you must be really careful what comes into it.

Think about it like this. When you get a burrito at your favorite taqueria, you know the game. You build the burrito by choosing the ingredients you'd like to go inside that flour tortilla. (By the way, have you checked out how many calories are in the tortilla alone? If not, don't look.) For me, I'm going to add steak, black beans, cheese, spicy salsa, guacamole, rice, and maybe even some veggies (making up for the tortilla). When it works like this, is it true I can choose what goes into my burrito? Yes! But once I put the burrito inside of me, I no longer have control of what it does to me. I'm simply at the mercy of the ingredients I've chosen to consume.

The lesson from this burrito illustration and from the Bible is this:

Whatever gets into you is going to spill out of you.

Jesus echoed the same thing:

No good tree bears bad fruit, nor does a bad tree bear good fruit. Each tree is recognized by its own fruit. People do not pick figs from thornbushes, or grapes from briers. A good man brings good things out of the good stored up in his heart, and an evil man brings evil things out of the evil stored up in his heart. For the mouth speaks what the heart is full of. (Luke 6:43–45)

While we want to be careful with what we put into us, we can also be careful about where we put ourselves. Environments matter.

Napa Valley has become a special place to me and my wife, Shauna. It is a life-giving and restorative setting that refreshes us so we can carry out our assignments in this season of our lives. We are blessed to live about an hour away from this beautiful place.

What has caused Napa Valley to become one of the leading wine destinations in the world? It's not just because there are great people who live and work there. It's not simply because of the amount of wealth there. It's not even because of its close proximity to San Francisco. Napa Valley has become one of the greatest wine regions in the world because of its *environment*. It has what is called a Mediterranean climate, which only 2 percent of the world possesses. The warm days, cool evenings, and dry summers make it the ideal environment for growing world-class grapes to produce world-class wine.

An environment includes the surroundings or conditions in which a person, animal, or plant lives or operates. The environments we place ourselves in are going to form the person we become.

Are your current environments helping you become the person you intend to be?

Psalms, the largest book in all of Scripture, has helped me become so much of the person I am today. Notice how the opening words have everything to do with environments. Psalm 1:1–3 reads,

> Blessed is the one
> who does not walk in step with the wicked
> or stand in the way that sinners take
> or sit in the company of mockers,

but whose delight is in the law of the LORD,
    and who meditates on his law day and night.
That person is like a tree planted by streams of water,
    which yields its fruit in season
and whose leaf does not wither—
    whatever they do prospers.

Which leads us to this principle:

There are some environments we need to remove ourselves from.

"Blessed is the one who does not walk in step with the wicked or stand in the way that sinners take or sit in the company of mockers." Notice the progression: Walk. Stand. Sit. Passing by to pausing to just taking a seat right in the middle of that kind of environment. The person who does not do this is blessed, in part because they have removed themselves from an environment opposed to God and his ways.

What environments do you need to remove yourself from?

Think about people. Who brings out the worst in you?

Think about places. Where do you go physically or even digitally that takes you away from God and his intention for your life?

Think about situations or activities. What are you doing that causes you to get further from God instead of drawing close to him?

What environments do you need to place yourself in consistently so you become the person you long to be?

It is so easy to be consumed with what we're meant to do with our lives. I love considering all the possibilities that could exist in the future. However, I want to encourage you to keep giving even more consideration to the person you're becoming. One of the best ways to keep yourself on the right path is by examining the why behind what you do.

NOTES

Are your current environments helping you become the person you intend to be?

_____

_____

_____

What environments do you need to remove yourself from?

_____

_____

_____

What environments do you need to place yourself in consistently so you become the person you long to be?

_____

_____

_____

2

Why and *How* Are Greater Than *What*

Whatever it is you will end up doing with your life, why you do it and how you do it will matter even more than what you do. Why do you do what you do? What are your motives? What are the reasons you live the way you live? Why do you spend money on the things you spend money on? Why do you volunteer at your church or another nonprofit organization? What is it you're really after?

The tricky thing about motives is they cannot be seen, at least not initially.

You could observe a parent doing a really good job of caring for their kids and yet have no idea why they are doing this. It could be they are parenting this way in public so you think they're a good mother or father. It could be they are doing it because they feel guilty for all the time they spend away from their children. Or it could be they care deeply for their children and are willing to sacrifice what they want for the sake of those kids.

Another thing we easily get wrong is when we judge someone based on the job they hold or the industry they work in. What comes to your mind when you think about people in the following professions? A lawyer. A teacher. A police officer. A pastor. It is easy to assume you know someone's motives without knowing anything about them personally. You might have a profession that makes people think you must care deeply for others. Or perhaps your job would make others predict you must not care too much about people. The truth is the motivation behind what you do is of greater importance than what you do.

Most of us believe we can look at someone's actions and automatically assume their motives are pure or impure. But we can't actually tell why someone is doing what they are doing.

I have already mentioned we started a church from scratch in downtown San Francisco. But why did we do that? That's a really good question and there are many possible answers. Was it so people would think God loves them, or was it so people would think I'm amazing? Was it so we could live in a really exciting city and this would help me escape the boredom I experienced in other places we'd lived? Did I do this to prove myself, knowing if I could start a church in a city like San Francisco, then surely I'd have the attention of leaders everywhere?

How about you? Why are you doing what you're doing?

Our motives really matter, and we aren't even always aware of our true motives. The fact that motives aren't easily detected by others means we could be doing what we're doing for all kinds of reasons. "All a person's ways seem pure to them, but motives are weighed by the LORD" (Prov. 16:2). We may be able to fool everyone else when it comes to our motives, but we will not be able to fool God. He sees us for who we truly are. And we don't want to fool ourselves.

Take a pause and really give the following question some thought. Read it out loud. Be as honest with yourself as you can.

Why are you doing what you're doing?

If we are going to talk about the why underneath all we do, we cannot leave this word out: ambition. The *Cambridge Dictionary* defines it as "a strong wish to achieve something."[1] So is ambition a good thing or a bad thing? Ambition is neutral. It doesn't have any morality in and of itself. It depends on who or what the ambition is for.

We're told to "do nothing out of selfish ambition" (Phil. 2:3). So many people seem to want to put themselves at the center of the world and ask everyone else to orbit around them. I think about people who are rich and make their wealth all about themselves. I think about people who are powerful and use their power for self-serving purposes. I think about people who have great privilege and utilize it only for their own benefit.

Instead, we're called to have ambition for God and for others. We need to look no further than Jesus to see how we should steward that. Jesus lived with a focused mission his entire life. However, his ambition wasn't for himself alone. He made it his aim to be ambitious for people just like you and me. He said as much in Mark 10:45: "For even the Son of Man did not come to be served, but to serve, and to give his life as a ransom for many." Before we start covering what God wants us to do with our lives, let me encourage you to adopt this mantra:

Whatever God wants me to do with my life, it will never be all about me.

Self-absorption never delivers what it promises. I'm guessing all of us have bought into the lie that making our lives all about us will somehow bring greater happiness. Self-care has become a priority for so many individuals, especially over the past decade. I think it's a wonderful thing, but I also think there's a huge difference between self-care and self-obsession. If you care about the mission God has given you, you'll want to prioritize taking care of yourself. If you don't take care of yourself, you can't take care of others. But if your purpose only involves taking care of yourself, you've missed the point of your life.

I love what Jon Tyson said about ambition when I interviewed him on the *Bring It Out* podcast: "Christians with torn ambition are a disaster in the world, but Christians with holy ambition have a complete and utter corporate advantage because they're willing to work hard without worldly recognition, for the good of others, and the glory of God. And that's an employee anybody will want on their team."[2]

Any conversation about whether our ambition is positive or negative will include the topics of pride and humility. I'm convinced so much of what we receive from God or miss out on from him will come down to those characteristics. God loves to help the humble, but he opposes the proud. Whether we choose humility or pride will lead to God fighting for us or against us.

What is it that feeds our humility? Recognizing that any good in our lives comes to us from the hand of God, either directly or indirectly. Remembering where our journey started increases the chances we will stay humble. If we will trace our accomplishments back to where they originated, eventually we will see they go back to something God has provided for us.

What has happened in your life that you could never take credit for?

Whatever that is for you, don't forget it. Write it down. Let me tell you what it is for me. Most Sundays you will find me on a stage in downtown San Francisco speaking to people who are intelligent and accomplished. You will rarely see me glance down at my notes, if ever. If you stand in the lobby with me after our services, you might hear people talk about how helpful that particular message was for their lives. (Of course, you might hear the exact opposite.) What would keep this from leading to pride in my life? Well, unlike most of those people, I know where this whole thing started.

I was a business major my freshman year of college. Every business major had to take an introduction class to public speaking. For our first speech, the professor asked us to prepare a five-minute speech on any topic of our choice. No big deal, right? Having been a baseball player in high school, I decided to give a speech on how to properly field a ground ball. I wrote the speech out. I went over it the night before I was supposed to give it, but I just couldn't go through with it. I chose not to go to that class—no, not just the next day . . . never again. I ended up withdrawing from the class, and shortly thereafter, I switched majors to something outside of the business school. I thought my only option was to major in something that would not require me to deal with public speaking ever again.

I wish I still had that sheet of paper declaring my withdrawal from that class. I could not stand up and give a five-minute speech about something I knew like the back of my hand. At the same time, I'm so grateful this is where my communication journey began. It reminds me that God is able to take an area of weakness and turn it into a strength. It also fuels my faith to believe other things are possible for my future, even if they seem impossible in the present.

When I'm tempted to become prideful because of how God uses this gift in my life, it's so helpful to remember this part of my story. Maybe that's why God is using this area in my life right now. He loves to work through the humble, and he allows the prideful to do things on their own—after all, that's kind of how they want it anyway. My story reminds me of the conversation between Moses and God in Exodus 4:10–12:

> Moses said to the LORD, "Pardon your servant, Lord. I have never been eloquent, neither in the past nor since you have spoken to your servant. I am slow of speech and tongue."
>
> The LORD said to him, "Who gave human beings their mouths? Who makes them deaf or mute? Who gives them sight or makes them blind? Is it not I, the LORD? Now go; I will help you speak and will teach you what to say."

Moses is going to approach the most powerful person in the world, and he knows he doesn't have the communication gift he needs. This will both keep him humble and cause him to rely on the strength that only God can provide.

What is in your story that should help keep you humble?

It is easy to start off humble but hard to stay that way. When we start something new, we don't have much of anything. We don't have a following. We don't have wealth. We don't have experience. We don't have influence. We don't have an audience.

I invite you to read the story of Uzziah in 2 Chronicles 26. I'll highlight a few of the things there as we think about how someone moves from humility to pride. When Uzziah is young, he does what is right in the eyes of God. As long as he seeks God, God gives him success. So you would think he would continue to seek God, but this isn't the case. In fact, we read these words in verse 16: "But after Uzziah became powerful, his pride led to his downfall."

Never forget where you started and that God has brought you this far.

One of the greatest learnings I've had over the past few years is how contentment and ambition work together. For so much of my life, my ambition was about my quest for contentment and fulfillment. I thought accomplishment would bring me joy. I assumed if I could just hit all my goals, then I would find guaranteed satisfaction. But I ended up learning this about the relationship between contentment and ambition:

Accomplishment Alone ≠ Long-Lasting Contentment

At first, it was painful to learn that no amount of success would ever help me find contentment. But then I learned a beautiful truth: I can have contentment and fulfillment without having to earn it through my success.

On the Enneagram, I'm a type 3, which is known as the Performer or the Achiever. This means when I'm unhealthy, my whole sense of identity has to do with what I've accomplished or produced. However, by God's grace, I began realizing he can bring me to a place of deep contentment that isn't dependent upon any level of success or failure I have in my life. Do you know how much freedom this has brought me and how much it can bring you?

You might think this discovery would lead me to having less ambition in my life, since I now know I don't need to go after something external to have the internal satisfaction I've always longed for. But it's actually done the opposite. When you no longer want or need to accomplish something for the sake of gaining contentment, you are free to make an even bigger impact. I know it sounds counterintuitive, so let me explain it using a formula:

Ambition + Godly Motivation + Heart for Others = Long-Lasting Contentment

Before I get to what you should consider doing with your life, I briefly want to touch on how you do what you do. Here's why I think this is important. If you do the right thing in the wrong way, something significant will still be missing from your life. In 1 Corinthians 10:31, Paul writes, "So whether you eat or drink or whatever you do, do it all for the glory of God." I love that Paul includes eating and drinking. It isn't just in the big things that we're to do what we do for the glory of God. This is to be the case in everything we do.

Let's be clear on one thing, however. There are some things we can never do for the glory of God. If we are engaged in any activity that God forbids, it would be impossible for us to bring him glory while doing it. Maybe the first place to start is by removing anything from our lives that can never be done for God's glory. Is there anything you're currently doing in your marriage or dating relationship that cannot bring God glory? Is there anything you're spending money on that can't be done with godly ambition? Is there any practice in your business that goes against the ethics God has clearly laid out?

Paul continues to instruct us on how we do what we do. In Colossians 3:23–24 he writes, "Whatever you do, work at it with all your heart, as working for the Lord, not for human masters, since you know that you will receive an inheritance from the Lord as a reward. It is the Lord Christ you are serving." So whatever you do, give it all you've got.

This reframes the kind of work we are doing in our lives. It also shifts how we do our work.

Whatever you do—big or small, in front of thousands or with no audience, whether you are getting paid or doing it for free—do it all for the glory of God, as though you were working for Jesus. What shifts would occur if you did everything in your life for the glory of God?

If you do the right thing but in the wrong way or for the wrong reason, it will have a devastating effect on you and other people. Whatever you're giving your time and energy to, it's helpful to examine your true motivation. I find it helpful to remind myself why I'm living out my God-given purpose in the first place. If your ambition has shifted in the wrong direction over time, confess it and ask God to purify your motives.

Now that we have clarity regarding our ambition, let's get into what we're actually called to do in this world.

NOTES

Why are you doing what you're doing?

_____

_____

_____

_____

What has happened in your life that you could never take credit for?

_____

_____

_____

_____

What is in your story that should help keep you humble?

_____

_____

_____

_____

3

Your *What* Really Matters

I think this is one of the most outrageous ideas God ever had:

God decided it would be great to get his work done on earth through people like me and you.

I don't know about you, but I'm not naturally good at delegation. It's a skill I've had to grow in, and I'm surrounded by people who are better than me at almost everything. So why would God delegate work to us that he could obviously do so much better himself? And how could Jesus have the audacity to say we would accomplish even greater things than he did during his time on earth (see John 14:12)?

The very first words of the Bible tell us that in the beginning, God was working. The second chapter tells us there was no one to work the ground. How exactly was the work going to get done? Was God going to do it all himself? Here's what he does, as stated in Genesis 2:15: "The LORD God took the man and put him in the Garden of Eden to *work it* and *take care of it*" (emphasis added). When God wanted to get work done on the earth, he gave an assignment to a human being. He is still getting his work accomplished in this way.

What work are we meant to do with our lives? When we typically think about the word "work," we often limit it to what we get paid to do. While this is a huge part of what we're supposed to do with our lives, we want to expand our vision for what else might be included in this concept. The word "vocation" encompasses all the stuff God has for us to do during our time on this earth. It comes from the Latin word *vocare*, which means "to call." So vocation is God-given, not self-appointed. I find great relief in knowing we don't have to call ourselves or come up with our own purpose in life.

Ephesians 2:10 tells us, "For we are God's handiwork, created in Christ Jesus to do good works, which God prepared in advance for us to do." If the God of heaven prepared specific good works for you to do, then you should do everything you can to discover what those works are. No matter how old or young you are. Regardless of whether you are male or female. Whether you have a past you're proud of or one you'd like to forget. No matter how other people have tried to define you. I want to encourage you to never lose sight of this as long as you live:

You have been given a divine assignment for your life.

Does God actually have a plan for your life? God says this to Jeremiah: "Before I formed you in the womb I knew you, before you were born I set you apart; I appointed you as a prophet to the nations" (Jer. 1:5). When you were born into this world, God was not caught off guard. He did not have to go scrambling to find some kind of purpose for you to fulfill with your life. God was thinking about you before you were born. The word translated "formed" has to do with what a potter

40

does with pottery. The idea is that a potter is shaping the clay for its intended use or purpose. Jeremiah is saying God had a purpose for you even before he formed you. Your life has been set apart and appointed for a purpose.

There is another moment in history that shows the pattern for how God tends to give us purpose. The Israelites (God's chosen people) had been enslaved for four hundred years in Egypt, under the rule of Pharaoh. God has had enough. He wants to do something about it. So he shows up in a burning bush to Moses. He lets Moses know he has seen all the misery his people have endured. He has listened to their cry for help and communicates his concern for their well-being. Then God declares he has "come down to rescue them from the hand of the Egyptians and to bring them up out of that land into a good and spacious land, a land flowing with milk and honey" (Exod. 3:8). He is coming to save them and bring them into a new land. God tells Moses what he is going to do. Moses has to be thinking, *That sounds great, God. Do it.* Then God says to Moses, "So now, go. I am sending you to Pharaoh to bring my people the Israelites out of Egypt" (v. 10).

What can this conversation between God and Moses teach us about our divine assignment? We have a purpose because God has a purpose. We are called to act because God wants to act. We have work to do because God has work to do. Our specific purpose is what God wants to get accomplished in the world through our lives.

The purpose for our lives originates in the heart of God. Our divine purpose will always be connected to God's purpose for a certain thing at a specific time.

Does the purpose you've assumed for your life seem to have originated in the heart of God?

Take a moment to pause and give serious reflection to the following questions.

What if our purpose doesn't start with what God wants *us* to do? What if our purpose begins with this question: What does *God* want to do?

When we give ourselves to living out God's purposes, we can live with greater confidence. In Psalm 33:11 we read, "The plans of the LORD stand firm forever, the purposes of his heart through all generations." The evil and injustice in our world do not change the fact that God has a purpose. The global pandemic of COVID-19 was incredibly challenging, but it did not negate God's ultimate purposes for the world.

As I'm writing this chapter, San Francisco looks like a much different city than when we arrived in 2010. While I don't know its future, I fully believe God has a purpose for this place and its people.

While you look to God to receive his purpose for you, you will also need his help and power to accomplish that purpose. I believe God wants to use you to change something about our world, but only in his strength and only for his glory. Whatever he wants to do through your life, you will be able to do it only through him.

To fulfill the divine purpose of your life, you need the divine presence in your life.

In the next chapter, we'll discuss how to figure out exactly what your God-given purpose is. Will you carry out whatever assignment God gives you?

So many of us are in search of our purpose. But if our purpose is the main thing we're after, then God simply becomes a means to an end for us. Don't get fixated with God's purpose for you if you aren't interested in what he wants to do with your entire life. As much as I want you to know your purpose,

I have an even stronger desire for you to know the giver of your purpose.

We do not have time to live out God's purpose and everyone else's.

Did you know God isn't the only one with a plan for your life? You likely have family members who have a plan for your life. Your boss could have a plan for your life. Scripture even says the devil has plans or schemes for your life. Our culture has purposes it wants you to carry out. It is so easy to get sucked into adopting the plans and purposes of everyone around us. This is why it's crucial to have the following rhythm in our lives: "Do not conform to the pattern of this world, but be transformed by the renewing of your mind. Then you will be able to test and approve what God's will is—his good, pleasing and perfect will" (Rom. 12:2).

Long before Moses had to decide whether he would carry out God's plans or give in to the plans of the world around him, there was a group of midwives facing the same choice. Exodus 1 tells us Shiphrah and Puah were the leaders of the midwives. Pharaoh had given the brutal order to kill all boys born to Hebrew women. Can you imagine the pressure these midwives were under? They had to make a decision—to follow God's ways or the powerful king's ways. They wanted to follow God's purpose, so they let the boys live. Not only did this go against the law at the time; it was also contrary to the cultural narrative they were surrounded by.

We are living in the middle of our own cultural narrative. And if we're being honest, sometimes it's just easier to go with the flow and practices of everyone around us. But if we live completely in step with the world, there's a good chance we're living out of step with the way of Jesus. I want to encourage us to adopt what I'm calling the Midwife Manifesto

as we consider what choices we're going to make with our
lives.

**To change your world, choose God's
ways over the world's ways.**

Help birth some new realities in the world.

**Choose the favor of God over the
favor of powerful humans.**

Jesus shows us how to stay committed to our heavenly Father's purpose, especially when everyone has ideas about what
our purpose in life should be. After Jesus's encounter with a
Samaritan woman at Jacob's well, the disciples return with
food and encourage him to eat. He responds by saying, "My
food . . . is to do the will of him who sent me and to finish his
work" (John 4:34). He makes his life about doing God's will
and finishing the work for which he was sent to earth. As his
life is concluding, listen in on what he says to God: "I have
brought you glory on earth by finishing the work you gave me
to do" (17:4).

Paul lives with a similar commitment. Hear from him as
he's being warned about what might happen to him if he keeps
moving forward: "I consider my life worth nothing to me; my
only aim is to finish the race and complete the task the Lord
Jesus has given me—the task of testifying to the good news of
God's grace" (Acts 20:24). His only aim is to finish the race God
gave him for his life. He isn't interested in coming up with his
own race to run in life. He isn't constantly comparing himself
to how everyone else is running their race. He's interested only
in finishing the race God gave him. Can we be content to make
it our only aim to do what God sent us to do while we're here
on earth?

I want this commitment for my life and I want it for yours. I pray my four children will give themselves to whatever God's purpose is for their lives. I want to be at peace with the part God has given me and cheer you on in the part he has given you. I believe God's power will show up in our lives in astounding ways as we simply say yes to whatever he has for us. I also believe giving ourselves to his mission will be the most satisfying thing we can do with our lives.

The world will tell you to keep aiming for the highest paycheck and the corner office. God will tell you the most significant thing you can do with your life is whatever he created you to do, which may or may not come with a corner office.

I have spent enough of my life trying to come up with my own purpose to pursue. I've also spent way too much time comparing myself to everyone else. It's exhausting wishing I had everyone else's assignment from God. Besides that, I would be miserable if I was trying to live out someone else's God-given purpose. God created me and gave me specific assignments for my life. He actually wants to get some of his work done through me. How amazing is that!

In the next chapter I will offer some practical wisdom on how to discover what your God-given purpose could be. But even before you know what it is exactly, let me encourage you to live with the faith that the God of the universe created you to do something with your life.

I want to offer a prayer for you to close this chapter. It's one I have often prayed for my life, my family, and our church. It comes straight from Scripture:

> The LORD will fulfill his purpose for me;
>   your steadfast love, O LORD, endures forever.
>   Do not forsake the work of your hands.
>   (Ps. 138:8 ESV)

NOTES

Does the purpose you've assumed for your life seem to have originated in the heart of God?

_____

_____

_____

_____

4

Design Alignment

We have now established the reality that God has a divine purpose behind your life. It begins in his heart, and he intends for you to accomplish some of his work during your time on this earth. You are in on this. You want what he wants. You are content to run the race he has called you to run. You want to echo the words of Jesus, that your food is to do the will of him who sent you and to finish his work (see John 4:34). But how do you distinguish a good idea from an actual calling? How do you know what your thing is in life or even for the next season of life?

There's a part of me that would love to tell you figuring out God's purpose for your life is a simple formula. But if it was, you would miss out on so much of the beauty of discovering why God has put you here on this earth. It's more of a dance than a formula. It's more trial and error than an exact science. However, you haven't been left in the dark. God isn't just out there waiting for you to catch up. He is with you as you seek to discover what he wants from your life.

Before we get into the specifics of your purpose, let's look at the general purpose of God for every person. When we talk about wanting to know God's will for our lives, what we typically mean is we want to know his specific will for our own lives. Where are we supposed to live? Who are we meant to marry? What kind of work are we to give ourselves to? What ministry is God asking us to be a part of?

While these specifics are extremely important, we often bypass the general purpose God has given to us. God wants all of us to know him and make him known to others. He wants us to orient our entire lives around Jesus. He wants all of us to produce the fruit of the Spirit in our lives. He wants us to love him with everything we have and to love our neighbor as ourselves. Whatever unique purpose God has for your life, it will not run contrary to his general purpose for all humans.

That being said, I do believe there are things you can do in your search to understand the God-given purpose for your own life.

Increase your God-awareness. If you want to know what God has sent you to this earth to do, it would help to get to know what this God is like. What does he value? What are his desires? How does he communicate with us? One of the best ways to discover what God is like is to have a consistent practice of reading, meditating on, and memorizing Scripture. This habit helps you to understand what God is like and how he operates. As you see how he revealed his purpose to individuals throughout history, you will get a sense of the possible ways he could do this in your own life.

On most mornings, I create space to read Scripture and pray. The reason I do this might surprise you. You might think I read the Bible every day because God speaks profoundly to me every day. That isn't the case. For starters, God has spoken through the pages of Scripture, so I know I'm hearing him in some way. But I also believe he can speak directly to me and my life in these times. I create this space every morning not because I know it's going to provide an "aha" moment for me to know my purpose. I create this space because, when the breakthrough comes, I don't want to miss it. Do you have a consistent pattern in your life for how you are continuing to become familiar with who God is and how he operates?

Increase your self-awareness. While it is crucial you get to know the God who made you, it is also essential you get to know the you this God has made. How has he wired you? What passions has he placed inside of you? What personality has he given you? What is your capacity? What makes you sad, happy, or angry? What talents and skills has God given you? These questions are helpful guides.

Also, what are you doing with what God has put in you? One of my favorite stories Jesus ever told is known as the parable of the talents (Matt. 25:14–30). In this story, a man entrusts various amounts of wealth to his servants. He gives five talents to one of them, two talents to another, and one talent to a third. (For reference, a talent was equal to twenty years of wages.) The first two invest what their master gave them and each double their initial amount. However, the third one hides what he was given because he's afraid.

Though this is a parable, there are principles we can extract from it. Here's the first one:

It is up to God what he gives you and how much he gives you.

God has not given us the same gifts or the same amount of gifts or even the same capacity within the gifts we share with each other. However, God gives each of us exactly what we need for what he has called us to do. Sometimes we feel responsible for what we cannot do, even if God never called us or gifted us to do it. But God wants you to do only what he has called you to. Stop feeling so much pressure thinking you need to be like someone else or do what someone else on Instagram is doing.

Here is an encouragement for all of us who can feel like we're not enough or we don't measure up: *Let's stop apologizing for the way God made us.* Think about this:

What God has given you is his gift to you. What you do with it is your gift to him and this world.

This has everything to do with the principle of stewardship. This word comes up a lot in conversations about money, but stewardship involves far more than what we do with our financial resources. It is a whole-life issue. Stewardship refers to the careful and responsible management of what has been entrusted to our care. Just like in the story Jesus tells, we are entrusted with different gifts and resources. Likewise, we will also be held accountable for what we do with what God has given to us.

Jesus gives us another principle in this parable. The master says, "Well done, good and faithful servant! You have been faithful with a few things; I will put you in charge of many things" (Matt. 25:21). So many of us are ready for a bigger platform and a higher position. Jesus seems to indicate if we will be faithful with where we are and what we have in this season, he might just give us more in the future.

Know your passions. What do you find yourself daydreaming about? What makes your heart start beating faster? What do you wish was different in our world? What brings tears to your eyes? What causes you to get excited? What are you doing when you experience a deep sense of fulfillment? What is it that breaks your heart? Oftentimes God gives us a passion for what he wants to accomplish in our lives.

I love the story of Nehemiah. It's fascinating to read about how he became laser-focused on what his God-given purpose was. When we are first introduced to him, we don't read anything about God telling him to return to Jerusalem and rebuild the wall around the city. We simply read that one of his brothers reports to him all that had happened in Jerusalem. His response will tell you how powerful our passions can be when it comes to our purpose: "When I heard these things, I sat down and wept. For some days I mourned and fasted and prayed before the God of heaven" (Neh. 1:4).

One fascinating thing I've noticed is how most of us want the rest of the world to be as passionate about the things we feel so passionate about. When we feel strongly about something, we think everyone else should feel just as strongly. Let me encourage you to stop wishing everyone cared as much about the things you care deeply about. That's not the way God intends for it to work. If you have a passion for something and it's a purpose that honors God, chances are he is wanting to use you to do something about it. Find a few others who do share your passion and go make a difference in the world together.

What is stirring in your heart these days? Is there anything you need to lean into, rather than away from, during this season? Is there something you just can't get off your mind? Does God seem to be speaking to you about the same thing over and over? What should you be getting involved in and doing something about?

Know your natural abilities. What have you discovered that comes really easy to you but not to everyone else? This is a great way to determine what abilities God has given you. What are you able to do that could make the most amount of difference in the world? This likely won't give you the entire answer to God's purpose for your life, but it will give you some things to consider.

When it comes to natural abilities, I want to include one disclaimer. I don't understand everything about this, as it has caused confusion for me at times. But I'll just go ahead and state it here:

Sometimes God's purpose for you is in an area where you have zero natural ability.

Moses wasn't a great speaker, but God called him to go to the most powerful person in Egypt and use his words. I do believe God primarily works through the abilities and skills he has given us. At the same time, I have seen enough occasions where someone was called to step into something that seemed to be well beyond what they were naturally good at.

Know your spiritual gifts. Scripture teaches that every Christian has at least one spiritual gift. There are a few prominent places in the Bible that detail this topic: Romans 12:3–8, 1 Corinthians 12, and Ephesians 4:11–13. These are not exhaustive lists, as they vary in terms of what they include. If you have never done a spiritual gifts assessment or if it's been a while since you've worked through one, I want to encourage you to find one online and go through it. Recognizing the spiritual gifts God has given to you is a great start. I also want to encourage you to both develop and deploy those gifts in your life.

Knowing my spiritual gifts hasn't given me a script to know my exact purpose, but it has aided me in the process so much. People think I'm joking when I mention I have only two spiritual gifts. But this is actually pretty close to the truth. My two primary spiritual gifts are teaching and leadership. I have many friends who have way more spiritual gifts than I possess. But I'm really thankful for the two God has given me. Knowing my gifts helps me stay focused on what I'm called to do in this world. It also eliminates me going after opportunities away from my gifts. I've made it my ambition to continue going deeper into these gifts. I want to become wiser and more skillful in how I use them.

What spiritual gifts has God given to you? What are you doing with them? Though there are exceptions, I believe we'll receive a direct blessing from God when we operate within our gifting. But it is important to remember this: a spiritual gift is operating properly only when God is producing something through us that we could never manufacture on our own.

Expect God to use anything and everything. I have tried to give you a few of the ways you can begin to understand your God-given purpose. You can also be confident God can and will use absolutely anything and everything to steer you toward his assignment for your life. He can use opportunities. He can redirect you if you end up on a path he doesn't have for you. He can use all kinds of circumstances to lead you into or out of something.

I see so many people put unnecessary pressure on themselves when it comes to knowing what God's purpose is for their lives. You don't have to do that, and it certainly won't help you out. If you keep getting to know God and keep getting to know yourself, increased clarity will come. Also, there will be times where God lets you make a choice. Don't freak out about the possibility of choosing the wrong thing. Keep becoming the right kind of person, and that will be enough. Stay patient and be content with small beginnings. Jesus waited thirty years before he stepped into the major purpose for which he was sent to earth.

Stop waiting for permission or certainty. So many of us are waiting for God to give us permission to act, while others of us refuse to move forward without having 100 percent certainty that we're doing the right thing. Paul knew his mission was to spread the message of Jesus. He believed he should do that in the most strategic places. I love how he didn't sit around waiting on God to tell him which city he should go to next. He knew his general purpose from God and he just went for it. He believed God could shut any door Paul wasn't supposed to be opening and was able to redirect him to the place he actually wanted him to go.

When you get some time, do a quick read of Acts 16:6–10. In verse 6, we see that the Holy Spirit keeps Paul from preaching the word in the province of Asia. Then Paul and his companions "tried to enter Bithynia, but the Spirit of Jesus would not allow them to" (v. 7). During the night, Paul has a vision of a Macedonian man asking for help. He concludes God is calling him to go share the message of Jesus in Macedonia. He doesn't wait for permission or certainty.

I see too many of us sitting on the sidelines until we are certain of what God is calling us to do. What if we allowed our current understanding of God's will for our lives to lead us forward? I'm afraid we've put so much pressure on ourselves to not get this wrong that oftentimes we do nothing . . . which is wrong. I know waiting on God is part of the process, but so is moving forward with God when it's time to go.

Let me share a bit of my story to illustrate this. I was serving as a teaching pastor in the Midwest when the idea of starting a church in San Francisco came into my heart and mind. I was doing a teaching series on the life of Esther. I love her story and how she had to decide to leverage her life for the sake of an entire community. My plan was to use this series to urge our church community to go for it—to be willing to do the hard thing and to lay their lives on the line if that was what it cost. I intended this message to be for everyone else in the room. But God intended it for me! This was when I began to seriously ask, "God, are you calling us to start a church somewhere?"

The three churches I had worked in had always been established churches in very specific locations. It's not like I could take those jobs and then determine exactly where I wanted to work. This calling was different. If I was going to start a brand-new church, I guess that could be done anywhere in the world. Based on how I believed God had wired me and thinking about how influence worked, I sensed God was calling our family to start a church in a major metropolitan area in the United States. With that in our minds and on our hearts, we considered five cities: New York, Boston, Chicago, San Diego, and San Francisco.

Out of all five possible locations, San Francisco was the only city I had never been to before. But as we prayed and did our research, everything kept pointing to the San Francisco Bay Area. Over time, I became convinced this was where God was leading us, but I didn't think we would end up in the city itself.

During the early days of prayer and research, two other couples agreed to be part of the team going to start this new church. When you pursue a major calling in your life, it really matters who is in it with you. The Lees and Milners, in my mind, were the right team to help us start the church. And I'm so thankful the Keels got on board and joined our team a few months later. In fact, I felt more sure about who we should do this with than even where we should do it. As you consider what God might be calling you into, who seem to be the perfect people to step into it with you?

The six of us (Pilgreens, Lees, and Milners) decided to plan a trip to San Francisco and the surrounding area in January 2009. Leading up to that trip, we took turns writing a fifty-day prayer guide. We were only going to have four days in California, and we really needed God to make it clear where this new church would be started.

On January 18, 2009, we landed at San Francisco International Airport. During our four days, we saw so many different communities. There were things about each of these places we really liked and felt drawn to. We had plans to spend one day in San Francisco. To be honest, this day was intended to be a fun time of being tourists in the big city. But God had other intentions. Isn't it amazing how we think something is going to go and then God shows us something we never would have expected? It became clear to all six of us that, indeed, God was calling us to start the church in the city of San Francisco. That would have been enough of a shock, but the specific call seemed to be leading us to downtown San Francisco. And our church, to this day, has always gathered in the same downtown neighborhood called SoMa (South of Market).

There were two things that gripped our hearts in that moment. First, we were convinced this was the place God was calling us to start the church. Second, we had no idea how it was going to happen. I think this is how a calling usually works. We become convinced God is leading us somewhere long before we have a clue how it's going to happen.

Some people never begin to pursue their calling because they can't yet see how it's going to become a reality. They get so obsessed with the how that they often set down the calling. Is there anything you aren't going after because you just don't see how it could ever happen?

If there's a grand designer behind your life, then it is worth exploring what he's designed you for. Let me encourage you to do everything you can to align yourself to God's purposes for your life. As author David G. Benner says, "Our vocation is always a response to a Divine call to take our place in the kingdom of God. Our vocation is a call to serve God and our fellow humans in the distinctive way that fits the shape of our being."[1] You were created for this. Your fulfillment will come from doing this. You will impact the world in a way you alone were designed to do. And my guess is you'll have a lot of fun along the way.

NOTES

My passions:

My natural abilities:

My spiritual gifts:

5

It's Not Too Late

If God has put a dream in your heart, I want to see it come out in your life. I know you do too. I also understand if you have some doubts about whether this can really happen for you. Maybe your current reality seems so far from the dream God put in your heart.

Before we dive deep into the principles that will help you live out your vocation, I want to urge you not to give up on the dream God has deposited inside of you. There are two major reasons we tend to give up on what God wants to bring out of us: We get tired of waiting for it to come out, or we feel like we've blown our chance to do what God called us to do.

When Joseph was seventeen years old, God gave him a dream. In this dream, he understood he was going to have some type of leadership position. How exciting! You can imagine how he began to think about his future and the high position he would be stepping into.

Every one of us knows what it's like to have dreams for our lives. We probably also know what it's like to see those dreams shattered. Joseph is hated so much by his brothers, they want him dead. Instead, they sell him to some Midianite merchants. And these merchants sell him to a guy named Potiphar, who happens to be one of Pharaoh's officials. While Joseph works for Potiphar, God gives him success and favor. In fact, he's given so much favor that Potiphar puts him in charge of his entire household. Potiphar's wife ends up accusing Joseph of doing something terrible he didn't do, and he gets thrown into prison.

This wasn't the dream. Egypt was not the dream. Thinking he would never see his father again was not the dream. Slavery was not the dream. Being falsely accused wasn't the dream. Prison wasn't the dream.

Have you ever been there? Divorce wasn't your dream. A health condition that has you seeing your doctor for weekly tests wasn't your dream. The company you started that still hasn't really gotten off the ground wasn't your dream. Being childless instead of having multiple children wasn't your dream. Anxiety and depression weren't your dream.

Are you living in the space between your dream and the fulfillment of it?

Joseph ended up in Egypt for a long time. Maybe you're in a place geographically or metaphorically you never imagined living. Are you somewhere in your life you never thought you would be? Does being in a different place than you thought lead you to think God is nowhere to be found?

One of the advantages we have with Joseph's story is we can see how it resolves. What causes us distress in our own story is we have no idea how it's going to end. Often quite a bit of time passes between when God gives us a dream and when he fulfills it. Don't walk away from your dream just because it hasn't been fulfilled yet.

What if your setback is actually a setup?

While Joseph is in prison, he interprets the dreams of two individuals. He asks one of them to remember him and mention him to Pharaoh, but this person forgets about him.

When things aren't going our way, we often think God has forgotten us. Let me remind you God has promised he is always with you. And if God is with you, he cannot forget you.

Finally, Joseph is remembered, and he becomes second in charge over Egypt. It doesn't happen overnight, but God is faithful to the dream he had given Joseph at age seventeen.

One day Joseph has a son, and I want you to see what he names him and why. "Joseph named his firstborn Manasseh and said, 'It is because God has made me forget all my trouble and all my father's household'" (Gen. 41:51). In faith, I want to believe a similar day is ahead for you. Don't lose heart. Don't walk off the path God has for you. He's going to bring out what he put inside of you. Please believe God has the ability to orchestrate the specifics of your life and your future.

Joseph later says to his brothers, "You intended to harm me, but God intended it for good to accomplish what is now being done, the saving of many lives" (50:20). When it seemed like nothing was going Joseph's way, God was positioning him for the future. We don't always know how God will use our present trials to set us up for the future.

If Joseph helps us to understand that dreams can be delayed, then Peter encourages us to overcome our own failures when it comes to stepping back into our purpose. When we're first introduced to Peter in Scripture, Jesus is inviting him and his brother Andrew to the grand mission of their lives. "'Come, follow me,' Jesus said, 'and I will send you out to fish for people'" (Matt. 4:19). Peter, having no idea what all this would mean, responds with immediate obedience. "At once they left their nets and followed him" (v. 20).

Do you remember the first time you heard God invite you to give your life to him and his mission? In that moment, you were convinced God made you on purpose, for a purpose. You were all in, fully committed to whatever work he had for you to do. You didn't care what it was, where it was, how much it paid, or what everyone else thought about it. You were convinced it was what you were put on this earth to do.

But something got in the way. Maybe it was a temptation or a trial. Perhaps it was multiple distractions that derailed you from the mission you were meant for. It could be that you got involved with the wrong group or you started isolating yourself from the kind of community you needed to stay on track. Maybe the allure of wealth or worldly status caused you to compromise your original commitment.

As I see it, there were two primary things that took Peter off the path intended for his life: control and fear. Jesus starts telling his disciples his mission will include suffering and resurrection. Peter has very different ideas about what the future will hold. "Peter took him [Jesus] aside and began to rebuke him. 'Never, Lord!' he said. 'This shall never happen to you!'" (Matt. 16:22). Peter wants to be in charge and call the shots. He wants to determine how it will all play out. As A. W. Tozer says, "Much of our difficulty as seeking Christians stems from our unwillingness to take God as He is and adjust our lives accordingly. We insist upon trying to modify Him and to bring Him nearer to our own image."[1]

Fear also causes Peter to walk away from his purpose. As things get more intense for Jesus, it has a profound effect on Peter. "Meanwhile, Simon Peter was still standing there warming himself. So they asked him, 'You aren't one of his disciples too, are you?' He denied it, saying, 'I am not'" (John 18:25). Fear leads Peter to deny he even knows Jesus.

I will spend an entire chapter on fear, but for now, I want to focus on how Peter is able to move forward from this massive failure.

Jesus suffers a horrible death on a cross, and three days later the resurrection takes place. When John 21 opens up, we see

Peter telling the other disciples he's going out to fish. What does this say about his assumption regarding his God-given purpose? He is going back to what he was doing before Jesus gave him his purpose. He thinks he has forever forfeited the purpose God had for him.

> **Have you returned to something from your past because you think your failure means you have to forfeit God's vision for your future?**

Jesus shows up to Peter and gives him a fresh calling. He's essentially telling Peter, "I still have a purpose for you. I still want to use your life. I still want you to impact others." Thankfully, Peter believes Jesus. He experiences a restoration of his faith. And less than two months later, he preaches to thousands of people about the death and resurrection of Jesus. He is able to tell them what is possible for their lives because he has experienced what is possible for his.

If this can happen for Peter, then it can happen for you too. I'm going to spend the rest of this book encouraging you to live out your God-given purpose. But that won't do you any good if you refuse to believe God still has a mission for your life.

Maybe you believe the dream for your life has died. If so, let me remind you—God loves to resurrect dead things. But even if your dream has died and the opportunity has passed, don't lose hope. God also loves to plant new things in us, including fresh dreams. The world is longing for your contribution. Your God is faithful. If your heart is still beating, then it's not too late. And I can't wait to see you bring out what I know is inside of you.

Before moving on, let me encourage you to offer this prayer:

God, I haven't always chosen to live for you and your purposes. I confess this to you and ask for your forgiveness. Restore our relationship and help me to believe you still want to use my life for your mission. As I experience your restoration, I make a fresh commitment to bringing out whatever you have put in me. Amen.

NOTES

Are you living in the space between your dream and the fulfillment of it?

What if your setback is actually a setup?

Have you returned to something from your past because you think your failure means you have to forfeit God's vision for your future?

Who Is Sitting at Your Wisdom Table?

Your future is going to be determined by the people seated at your wisdom table.

6

The Concept of a
Wisdom Table

I want you to think about your life as occurring across a number of tables. It will help you to actually picture these tables. You have your family table, and you can't really change who gets to sit at that one. Who all is seated there? This could include your immediate family or your extended family.

You have your work table, but unless you're the boss, you don't get a total say on who sits at that one either. Who are the people sitting at your work table? This could be the entire company if it's new or somewhat small, it could be the people in your department, or it might just be the team you're a part of within the department. If you happen to be self-employed or an entrepreneur who works alone, it's a table for one.

Hopefully you have a table of friends and no one is sitting there unless you want them to. Unless you live in isolation, you likely have a table of neighbors. While you can complain about the person who is loud or refuses to take care of their lawn, I'm guessing you don't get to choose your neighbors.

While all these tables are important in our lives, I want to introduce you to the table I think is the most important. Maybe you're already waging an argument with me before I even tell you what this table is exactly. Perhaps you would like to argue your family table has to be most important. Or I'm foolish not to put your faith table as the most important one. You might want to argue for your relationship table or your friendship one. You could even want to challenge me by saying your parenting table is the one deserving of your highest priority. Each of these is a significant table in your life, but what if I could give you one that has the potential to affect all the others in your life?

Your wisdom table is the most important table in your life.

Whoever is currently sitting at your wisdom table will determine so much about your life. This table will determine who is at your relationship table and how you live within your relationships. It will lead to how you engage your coworkers and your neighbors. Getting the right people at your wisdom table could even lead to financial prosperity, while getting the wrong people there could lead to financial ruin. If you have the right people there, you might become an amazing mom. If you have the wrong people influencing your parenting, perhaps you will raise kids who will one day want nothing to do with you. Get the right people around you, and your faith in God will likely be much stronger. Surround yourself with those who lack true wisdom, and you might be convinced you don't really need God in your life. I cannot overstate how crucial your wisdom table is for your life.

Nearly every for-profit business and nonprofit organization has some kind of board of directors. In the best organizations, a board is there to advise, make decisions, and hold individuals accountable to lead the company in the best possible way. The most helpful boards are those made up of people who are able to provide wisdom and insight for running the company, school, church, or other type of organization. If a major company refused to have a board or filled the board seats with those who lacked vital wisdom for running the business, we would all think that was a foolish decision.

Now I want you to think about something much more valuable to you than any organization in the world—*your life*. If we think it's foolish when a company places individuals on its board who lack the wisdom needed to navigate the future of the company, what do we call it when we seat people at our wisdom table who have no business being there? We should think that is foolish as well.

What if you began to think about assembling a personal board of directors for your life? This is exactly what I'm getting at when I refer to a wisdom table. Every single one of us needs a group of people who can serve as advisers and hold us accountable. We all need people who have wisdom for the specific things taking place in our lives. If you were putting together a personal board of directors for your life, who might you ask to serve on it? We will answer that in a moment, but I first want to show you the difference between a helpful wisdom table and a disastrous one.

Solomon, who was known as the wisest person to ever live, died around 930 BC. Rehoboam, his son, ascends to the throne and becomes king. His coronation is to take place in Shechem. While there, Jeroboam, who had worked for Solomon but eventually led a revolt against him, comes to Rehoboam and speaks on behalf of the people: "Your father put a heavy yoke on us, but now lighten the harsh labor and the heavy yoke he put on us, and we will serve you" (1 Kings 12:4). Rehoboam responds by telling all the people to go away and come back in three days.

In the meantime, Rehoboam consults the elders (think advisers) who served Solomon during his lifetime. He asks them a great question: "How would you advise me to answer these people?" (v. 6). I love that Rehoboam is humble enough and wise enough to seek the advice of others who have the experience he is lacking. They tell him, "If today you will be a servant to these people and serve them and give them a favorable answer, they will always be your servants" (v. 7). They give him great advice about how he can lead the nation as he steps into his kingship.

I wish I could tell you he kept these elders at his wisdom table and did everything they told him to do. "But Rehoboam rejected the advice the elders gave him and consulted the young men who had grown up with him and were serving him" (v. 8). This is so tragic to me, and yet I see people doing this all the time in our world today. Rehoboam has access to actual wisdom. He has a group of experienced advisers who are willing to serve him and help him in any way they can. But Rehoboam rejects their advice! Let that sink in.

You can have access to wisdom and
still not act on that wisdom.

Rehoboam removes the elders from his wisdom table and gives their positions to the friends he grew up with. Don't get me wrong, I'm sure he and his friends had a ton of fun growing up together. (Just imagine what it would have been like to grow up as Solomon's son or even to be a friend to his son.) I'm grateful for my childhood friends, but I'm not sure that automatically qualifies them to sit at my wisdom table today.

Rehoboam asks these childhood friends how they would advise him. They respond by saying, "These people have said to you, 'Your father put a heavy yoke on us, but make our yoke lighter.' Now tell them, 'My little finger is thicker than my father's waist. My father laid on you a heavy yoke; I will make it even heavier. My father scourged you with whips; I will scourge you with scorpions'" (vv. 10–11).

Rehoboam rejects the advice given him by the elders and follows the advice of his young friends. He dismisses wise people from his wisdom table and instead opts to put fools in their place. Here's the problem with doing this. If you put all fools at your wisdom table, then everyone is likely to be in agreement about how you should handle a given situation. And when everyone sitting there is in full agreement, you become convinced that solution must be the wisest one. In reality, that couldn't be further from the truth. When foolish people all agree on a course of action, then the decision is probably the most foolish one to make.

What does this foolish decision by Rehoboam lead to? "After Rehoboam's position as king was established and he had become strong, he and all Israel with him abandoned the law of the LORD" (2 Chron. 12:1). There are many things that likely led to this happening. But I think it can be traced back to what Rehoboam did with his wisdom table.

As you think about your future, what if the same is true when it comes to what you do with your wisdom table? Proverbs 13:20 says, "Walk with the wise and become wise, for a companion of fools suffers harm." Who's walking the path of life with you?

One of the most disheartening things I have observed is who people let sit at their wisdom table. When I see people I care about taking relationship advice from someone who has sabotaged every relationship they have ever been in, I want to say, "Please don't." When I see people in our church taking advice about spiritual growth from people who talk a big faith game but don't live it out, I want to say, "They aren't who you think they are." When I notice friends taking on the financial habits of those who are foolish with their money, I want to scream, "Please stop!"

We must be careful about who we allow to sit at our wisdom table. In the next few chapters, I want to cover some practical help as it relates to your wisdom table. Who should be sitting at it? How do you invite the right people? How should you dismiss the people who don't belong there? And what do you actually do with the people once they're sitting at your wisdom table?

NOTES

Who is currently at your wisdom table?

7

Who Belongs?

I hope you are convinced by now your wisdom table is the most important table in your life. It has the ability to bring much joy or much sorrow. We've learned some disheartening truths from an ancient king's story, and we realize how prevalent they are in our world today. Assuming you are committed to building the best possible wisdom table for your life, I want to help you understand exactly what you're looking for as you build it.

To construct a wisdom table that will help you thrive in every area of your life, it's crucial to learn what wisdom is. Some people think wisdom is synonymous with knowledge. It is not less than knowledge, but it is so much more. It refers to action, skill, or applied knowledge. Eugene Peterson said, "Wisdom is the art of living skillfully in whatever actual conditions we find ourselves."[1] Knowledge might help you pass a test in school, but wisdom will help you respond effectively to the specific challenges that will show up in your life.

I used to assume the most intelligent people in our world were by default also the wisest. I no longer think that, and I will tell you why. I have now lived in San Francisco more than a decade. Never in my life have I been around more intelligent, educated, and accomplished individuals. In the early days of our church, I often found myself a bit intimidated by the kinds of people who were showing up. It seemed like everyone had gone to an Ivy League school, Stanford, or UC Berkeley. I remember asking Shauna one day, "Why are all of these people showing up at Epic?" I knew they weren't there because they were looking to gain mere academic information. They were looking for wisdom. They wanted to know how to navigate the season of life they found themselves in, and their IQ alone wasn't able to give them the answers they were searching for.

The book of Proverbs is known as wisdom literature, meaning it isn't a historical account or a book about prophecy. It tells us how to think about living in God's world, in God's ways. These proverbs are not necessarily promises; they're more about probability. They focus on the general rule, but they don't include the exceptions. The writings in Proverbs are intensely practical. They cover so many topics, including marriage, friendship, sex, work, laziness, and finances.

There are three main characters introduced in the opening passage of Proverbs. Remember, it isn't history, so I don't mean there are three specific human beings introduced here. The three characters are known as the wise, the simple, and the foolish.

The wise person is the one who is making good progress in the skill of wisdom and whose example is worth following. They are always positioning themselves to gain wisdom. They see God and his ways as the source of wisdom.

The simple person is someone who is naive and untaught. This person's exposure to life and wisdom has been limited. The simple can be gullible, and they are easily influenced or misled.

The fool is someone who despises wisdom and instruction. The fool is steadily opposed to God and his ways.

Whether you are the wise, the simple, or the foolish isn't based on your education, accomplishments, or wealth. Wisdom can actually lead to all three of those, but none of them will guarantee that you have wisdom.

Proverbs 4:7 says, "The beginning of wisdom is this: Get wisdom. Though it cost you all you have, get understanding." The wisest thing you can do with your life is to gain wisdom, no matter what you have to pay for it. Wise people know how to navigate life when there is no formula to be found.

One of the best places to gain wisdom should be your wisdom table. But who belongs at this all-important table?

Consider those who see God as the ultimate source of wisdom. Everyone sitting at your wisdom table has an ultimate source they look to in their lives. This is true when it comes to what they value. It's true when it comes to the things they center their lives on. And it's true when it comes to the ultimate place they look to gain wisdom for their lives (and for your life, by the way). It's important to see God as the ultimate source of our wisdom and request the same of those who will occupy seats at our wisdom table. If God is the creator of our purpose and the wisest being in the entire universe, it makes sense he is the originator of our wisdom also.

If someone doesn't recognize that God is the source of all wisdom, they probably don't belong at your wisdom table. I say "probably" because I believe God can still give his wisdom even to those who refuse to acknowledge him in their lives. I would, however, use extreme caution if you're considering putting a person at your wisdom table who does not have faith in God. This doesn't mean my dentist can't give me wisdom about my teeth if he isn't a Christian. It just means I probably shouldn't give him a seat at my wisdom table.

You might now be thinking, *Okay, all I need to do is find some Christians and get them to my table.* Please don't do that; there are other qualifications they need to meet.

Make sure you see the fruit of their wisdom. If you can observe the fruit of someone's wisdom, they likely make a great candidate for your wisdom table. I've met many people who have theories on wisdom yet often don't apply this wisdom to their own lives. I've met others who have all kinds of thoughts on wisdom but don't have the experience to back up those ideas.

In the world we're living in today, it seems anyone can become an "expert" on whatever topic they choose. They can write a book, have many followers on social media, and offer their opinion on an unlimited number of topics. Before you ask someone to take a seat at your wisdom table, observe the fruit of their wisdom. You can do this by looking at their relationships, their work, their character, and the kinds of decisions they make.

Invite those who genuinely want what's best for you. You should never put someone at your wisdom table who doesn't have your best interests in mind. I'm not talking about having yes-men and yes-women who will go along with whatever you propose. That won't be helpful either. I'm talking about people who genuinely love you, and because they love you, they will always be willing to tell you the truth. Surround yourself with individuals who truly want good for you and are committed to helping you thrive in life. You cannot put people at your wisdom table if they are afraid to be honest with you. It is best to find people who will live out the combination of both encouragement and challenge in your life. So much of the growth in my life can be attributed to being challenged by people who I know have my best interests in mind.

Maybe you're now so afraid of having the wrong people at your wisdom table that you are considering not having anyone seated there. You think, *I'll just figure out life and faith and relationships and work on my own.* But as Proverbs 12:15 says, "The way of fools seems right to them, but the wise listen to advice." You and I need others who can see what we cannot see. I have blind spots and so do you. A fool says, "It looks right to me, so let's go with it." A wise person says, "It looks right to me, but let me ask a few other wise people if they see it the same way."

I am incredibly grateful for the people who have been at my wisdom table throughout my life. And I am especially humbled by the individuals who are currently seated there. These are people who have a passion for Jesus and continue to cultivate their relationship with him. They also happen to be people with a wisdom track record. I can see the fruit of their wisdom. I've met their families and noticed the way they handle their finances. I have seen them act in humility when their accomplishments could have led to pride. For the ones who are married, I see the way they honor and respect their spouses.

These people also want what's best for me. This means they don't just ask how the church is growing. They ask me about my kids or my marriage or about my own growth and development. And they have no problem telling me when they see something in my life that needs correction. I can't imagine what I would be doing without them.

Now I want to help you think of customizing your own personal board of directors. To think about your specific wisdom table, let me walk you through some possible categories for your life.

Spiritual Life. How would you describe your current location on your faith journey? Based on where you are, who would make sense to put at your wisdom table? If you're new to Christianity, maybe you would want to seek out someone who has been a committed Christian for a number of years. If you are wanting to grow in a particular spiritual practice, seek out someone who has wisdom in and experience with that practice. If you want to reach your non-Christian friends in a winsome way, it seems wise to seek the wisdom of someone who has had a major influence on their friends and colleagues coming to faith in Jesus.

Spiritual formation is something I care deeply about. When I notice someone who seeks God consistently and has strong character, I'm very curious as to how that was formed in them. I want to seek those kinds of people to sit at my wisdom table. Who do you want speaking into your spiritual life?

Relationships. What's your current relationship status? Are you single, dating, engaged, married, widowed, or divorced? Whatever relational season you are in, invite someone with the appropriate wisdom to speak into your life. If you are engaged, find wise couples and ask them to pour their wisdom into your relationship.

Shauna and I are blessed to have a number of couples at our wisdom table. We want couples who are ahead of us in life. When we meet healthy couples who have been married for over thirty years, we long to know their secret. As you think about who you currently take wisdom from in the relational area, would you like to end up with the kinds of relationships those people have? If so, there's a good chance you should keep them at your wisdom table. If not, find people who can speak into your relationships and whose relationships you want to emulate.

Friendships. In addition to romantic relationships, healthy friendships can be a great source of joy in our lives. Find individuals who seem to have deep and long-lasting friendships. Ask them how those relationships began and how they've been sustained over the years. Tell them what challenges you face when it comes to forming your own friendships.

Parenting. I realize you might not be a parent, and if that's the case, feel free to move on to the next area of life. But if you do have kids, I hope you want as much wisdom as possible when it comes to raising your children. Who around you seems to be doing a superb job of raising their kids or perhaps has already raised their children? These are the people you want to seek a meeting with or reach out to over the phone. Ask them questions like these: *What are your secrets to great parenting? What are the rhythms you have with your family? How does discipline work in your home? How much freedom did your kids have at a specific age?* When I ask these kinds of questions, I tend to get very specific answers. Occasionally someone will reply, "I don't know if we really had a plan." If you get this response, don't end the conversation there. Chances are high they actually did have a plan, and if you ask enough questions, you'll be able to recognize some specific things they implemented.

Shauna and I have some friends who are a few years ahead of us in the parenting game. Here's why these tend to be the people I seek out most for my wisdom table: I prefer to have people who are ahead of me but not too far removed from the situation I'm currently navigating with my own children.

Vocation. What is your current job or your current unpaid vocation? What is your industry? What size is the company or organization you work for? What is your position? What are the things you need to learn in this next season to be productive and successful? Find people who are doing what you are or want to be doing, and invite them to sit at your wisdom table. If you want to start your own business, find some wise entrepreneurs who have already done what you're attempting to do. If you're considering changing industries, it seems wise to find some people who are in that profession, and it's probably best to do so before leaving your current one. If you want to know what it takes to be a great executive, can you guess who you should ask? That's right—an amazing executive whose wisdom you can observe.

Finances. God really cares about what you do with your financial resources, and so should you. Perhaps in this area of life more than any other, God's wisdom could not be further from the wisdom of this world. We all need people with financial wisdom to sit at our wisdom table. We need to learn how to think about money. It should be our aim to be strategic with what we spend, what we invest, what we save, and what we give.

What's your current financial reality? What kind of person do you need to gain wisdom from in this season? If you're in debt, find someone who has overcome debt or someone who is able to show you how to overcome it. If you make way more money than you know what to do with, find someone who can help you think strategically about your habits when it comes to generosity.

I have a few different people at my wisdom table who speak into my financial situations. One person encourages me to think creatively about my generosity. Another helps me with investment advice. And I love asking this question of my mentor, who is twenty-five years older than I am: "What should I be doing at my current age to position our family for the future?"

Unique Projects. You will inevitably find yourself in a season where you need some wisdom for a unique project. This could include almost anything, from home repairs to how to plan for a sabbatical to how to think about the college selection process for your firstborn child. It's okay to give "seasonal" passes to your wisdom table. I don't know about you, but I always want to find the wisest people I possibly can when it comes to filling these unique seats at my wisdom table. So how do you find them? Start asking people you know questions like, "Do you know anyone who is great at _____?" As you gather a list of possibilities, offer to take those people to coffee. Be willing to meet with them at their convenience, rather than forcing them to meet at yours. After all, you are the one in need of their wisdom.

When I sensed God leading me to start a church in San Francisco, I knew I needed a massive amount of wisdom. At the end of 2008, I was introduced to Andy Wood, who started Echo

Church in the San Francisco Bay Area. I am not exaggerating when I say this one introduction changed the trajectory of my life, my leadership, and Epic Church. Andy is one of the greatest leaders I've ever met, and for some strange reason, he was willing to invest in me. I had never started a church before. He had already planted one church and was months away from starting another one in the same area where God was leading us to start a church. He would tell me what he was reading, who he was learning from, and what conferences he was attending. He would send me his notes of the things he was learning. He helped me think about raising funds, putting together a team, finding a facility, and everything else that comes with starting a church.

Andy ended up introducing me to Rick Burge, who helps oversee church planting for Lake Pointe Church in the Dallas area. After Rick and I got to know each other, he introduced me to Steve Stroope, who led Lake Pointe for forty years.

When I think about all God has done in my life and in our church, these three men immediately come to mind. Having these guys sitting at my wisdom table has brought so much blessing into my life. I cannot imagine what I or our church would have missed out on if they weren't there. The number of calls we've had. The number of decisions they've spoken into. The number of ideas they've caused me to consider. The way they've helped me position Epic Church to own property in San Francisco. How they've encouraged me to be a better husband and father. The hard and joy-filled moments we've shared with each other.

I could go on and on, but let me say this to you as I think about my own wisdom table:

*If you get the right people at your wisdom table,
they will change the trajectory of your life.*

NOTES

Think about each person currently at your wisdom table. Are they wise, simple, or foolish?

Which categories do you want to fill at your wisdom table?

8

Term Limits

I have tried to make the case that it really matters who gets invited to sit at your wisdom table. However, it is equally important who is *not* going to sit there. So what do you do when you need to disinvite people from your wisdom table? To disinvite someone means to withdraw or cancel their invitation. Before you start getting nervous, don't worry. You do not have to tell someone they are no longer invited to sit at your wisdom table. You just quit asking their advice, or if they insist on still giving you their "wisdom," you ignore it.

> **Who is currently sitting at your wisdom table that should no longer have a seat?**

Here are some areas to consider.

Those whose fruit has disappeared. Let's assume there was a time in your life when you built the ideal wisdom table. You put people at it who saw God as the source of all wisdom, you could see the fruit of their wisdom, and you knew they wanted what was best for you. You made sure to put people there who could give you great advice about your spiritual life, your relationships, your parenting, your vocation, and your finances. I wish you could just get this right one time and it would serve you for life. Unfortunately, that's not going to be the case.

Even if someone has a stellar track record when it comes to their wisdom, do not give them a lifetime appointment at your wisdom table. Continue to pay attention to the life they are currently living, not simply how they used to live. To illustrate this point, let's think about Solomon. He's known for being the wisest person to have ever lived. And God is the one who gave him his wisdom. If you were building your wisdom table back then and you had access to Solomon's wisdom, you would have made him your first draft pick. "When all Israel heard the verdict the king [Solomon] had given, they held the king in awe, because they saw that he had wisdom from God to administer justice" (1 Kings 3:28). Who wouldn't want this guy sitting at their wisdom table?

But there came a day when Solomon stopped leaning into the wisdom God had made available to him. He began to love many foreign women, even though this was against what God had told the Israelites to do. The end result of this decision was tragic. "As Solomon grew old, his wives turned his heart after other gods, and his heart was not fully devoted to the LORD his God, as the heart of David his father had been" (1 Kings 11:4). If Solomon had been at your wisdom table, would you have been willing to dismiss him after this moment? I pray you'll have people at your table who will go the distance when it comes to being men and women who are full of wisdom. But if there comes a day when they no longer fit the criteria, be brave enough to dismiss them from your wisdom table . . . because your future depends on it.

Those whose wisdom you have outgrown. Most people at your wisdom table probably won't be there forever. I want to show you how to recognize when their season ends, how you can navigate it, and how to provide closure that will be a blessing to them.

God has blessed me with so many people who were exactly the right ones I needed in a given season. I think about the woman who gave me my first job in full-time ministry. I was clueless and she taught me so much. I think about the man who first introduced me to the concept of leadership. This one piece of wisdom began a journey for me that has paved the way for so much of what I'm doing these days. I fondly recall people who first helped us acclimate to life in San Francisco. I have learned so much from these people and many others, and I am profoundly grateful. But some of these individuals are no longer at my wisdom table. They didn't do anything wrong. Nothing happened between us that was negative. It's just that they don't have the experience or wisdom to speak into what I'm currently doing in my life and leadership.

Seasons come and go. Most people will be needed at your wisdom table only for a season. It could be because you are dealing with a specific challenge or opportunity. Once you have worked through that particular issue, there might not be another compelling reason to have those people at your wisdom table. For others, there might come a day when your wisdom surpasses theirs in a certain category. You do not need to feel guilty about this, but there is something you need to do. If the day comes when you have outgrown the wisdom of someone who has been a vital part of your advisory team, go above and beyond to express thanks to them. Even if it's been years since they provided wisdom to your life, I encourage you to find time this week to express your gratitude to them. You can write a card or a letter. You can make a phone call. You can give a unique gift that will express how beneficial they have been to your life. It's okay to move on and welcome new people in their place, but not before you adequately recognize all the good they have brought into your life.

Family. Many of us assume the people sitting at our family table should automatically be given a seat at our wisdom table. It would be such a blessing if those at your family table were the kind of people who should also occupy a spot at the most important table in your life. Unfortunately, that won't be the case for many of you. How can you objectively know whether or not family members should have a seat at your wisdom table? I use the word "objectively" because there are so many thoughts and emotions tied to anything that has to do with our family of origin. To be objective, use the filter we learned in the last chapter to ask these questions: Do they view God as the ultimate source of wisdom? Are you able to see the fruit of their wisdom? Do these people, regardless of your biological relationship to them, have your best interests in mind?

While family can refer to anyone you are related to, the most challenging people you may ever have to dismiss from your wisdom table will be your parents. On the one hand, you know you are meant to love, honor, and respect them. These directives are for all of us. On the other hand, what do you do when you realize their beliefs and opinions might lead you down a path that isn't best for what God has for your life? If your parents' marriage isn't one you want to imitate, it's probably best not to gain relational wisdom from them. If you see a lack of integrity in the way your father runs his business, I'm not sure you should get his wisdom on how you approach your own job. If you see a pattern of self-obsession in your mother's life, I'm guessing you might not want her advice on how to become more selfless in your own life.

I've been amazed to discover how much power one or both parents can still have in the lives of adults in their thirties and forties. Over the past few years, I've found myself in meetings with very accomplished people. On the outside, they seem to have it all together, and I wonder why they want to meet with me. On most occasions, these are individuals who attend our church. After a bit of small talk, they will tell me how one of their parents isn't pleased with a choice they've made, which usually comes from one of these categories: who they married, the kind of career they have, where they live, how they're raising their kids, or something involving their faith. You would be surprised by the number of adults who have felt God calling them to be baptized as a way of identifying with their Christian faith, but to do so meant they had to get over the disapproval of their parents.

What do you do in these kinds of moments? Perhaps you believe God is calling you to take a step in your relationship with him, and yet, this step could have a negative impact on your relationship with your parents. They will always be your parents, but they no longer need to stay at your wisdom table.

When you no longer think your mother or father needs to be sitting at your wisdom table, how do you move forward? You keep loving them. You keep investing in the relationship. You pray for them. You make time to call them and arrange to visit them, unless it would be toxic to do so. You do nothing to spite them. I would also encourage you to do this if possible: find one area where your mom or dad has some knowledge. It could be about cooking or cars or the stock market or some hobby. If you are able to find an area like this, position yourself to ask for their insight as much as possible. But don't give them a seat at your wisdom table.

Before I leave this section, I imagine you might be wondering if my parents have a seat at my wisdom table. My mom died of cancer when she was forty-six and I was twenty-five. My father has given me so much wisdom throughout my life and continues to do so at the time of this writing. I've gained wisdom from him on becoming a man after God's own heart. He has helped so much in building my character. He's shown me what it looks like to be generous with all God has blessed me with and so much more. (I promise I'm not saying this just because I think he will read my book.) I actually spoke with my dad about twenty minutes ago. I was asking for his prayers as I write this book, and he gave me more of his wisdom: "Don't force it. Just let it come to you." Thanks, Dad.

Friends. Friendship is one of the greatest gifts a person can enjoy in life. I hope you have a few true friends. I say "few" because I don't think it's possible to have many deep friendships. When it comes to your closest friends, it's quite possible you have given them a seat at your wisdom table without doing a full vetting process. Just because you are friends with someone doesn't mean they are necessarily full of wisdom. You could be friends because you've known each other since childhood. Perhaps the two of you met when you were in the same sorority at the university you attended. Maybe you hit it off at CrossFit. You could have formed the friendship because the two of you have so much in common. Maybe they're a person who is just a lot of fun to be around. Celebrate that you have a friend like this.

But when it comes to whether or not this friend deserves a seat at your wisdom table, you must apply the same criteria we've been learning about. A person who is a train wreck when it comes to personal finances can still make a great friend (as long as they aren't always asking you for cash), but do you really want their advice when it comes to your financial habits? Someone who has ruined every romantic relationship they've ever been in can still be a ton of fun to spend time with, but do you really want dating or marriage advice from them? Don't let someone have a seat at your wisdom table just because they've been at your friend table for so long. In fact, what would be amazing is if they could see the value in asking *you* to sit at *their* wisdom table.

Boss. If you want to keep your job, it's probably a good idea to do the tasks and work projects your supervisor assigns to you. Just because they are a level above you, however, doesn't mean they are wiser than you. In fact, their having a certain position within a company or organization never ensures they are a wise person. My hope is you work for someone who can be a great source of wisdom in your life. It would be amazing to have a boss who not only gives you advice for work but offers wise counsel in other areas of your life as well. However, don't assume they should have a seat at your wisdom table just because they have a nicer office and a larger paycheck than you do. By the same token, people at a lower level could be great sources of wisdom in your life. Ask yourself, *Has God given me a supervisor or some other colleague who makes a great candidate for my wisdom table?*

Church Leader. I wish I didn't have to include this one. I would love to be able to tell you any church leader you have access to should have a guaranteed seat at your wisdom table. Unfortunately, I have seen so many people assume their pastor or small group leader should be given a seat at their table without doing a thorough investigation. For starters, let me encourage you to be part of a church where God's wisdom is sought and taught. I'm not suggesting you put every church leader on trial, but I do think you should be able to observe the fruit of their wisdom. Do they seek the wisdom of God? Do they make decisions that are good for the community? Do they have a healthy marriage or other healthy relationships if single? Do they want the best for you? If not, be careful you don't give them a seat at your wisdom table. If you are attending a church where the wisdom of God isn't sought or taught, I would recommend you find a place where that is happening. And regardless of what your experience has been so far, I know for a fact there are many church leaders out there who would be an added blessing to your wisdom table.

How should you handle a resignation from your wisdom table?

This one is personally the hardest for me. You have a person who, in the past, has been willing to spend time with you and dispense wisdom into your life. But for some reason, they no longer make themselves available or accessible to you.

God sent a person into my life during a crucial season of leadership. We had a mutually beneficial relationship. We spent time together at least twice a month. On top of that, we would exchange text messages and have phone calls fairly often. I made sure to express to him how grateful I was for the wisdom he gave me. And then one day, it all changed. I couldn't get any time with him. He rarely answered or even returned my calls. I asked him if there was anything I had done and received no response. I was hurt, and perhaps the most frustrating thing was the fact I had no clue as to why things changed. I still don't know.

What do you do in a situation like this? You do what you can, but you realize you can't make anyone stay at your wisdom table.

I decided to write a note to this person to accomplish two things. First, I wanted to apologize in case I had done something I wasn't aware of. Second, I expressed my gratitude for the role he had played in my life during the time he sat at my wisdom table. I believe expressing gratitude is the most important thing we can do to keep bitterness from taking up residence in our hearts. And who knows . . . hopefully by the time you're reading this, I'll have an old friend sitting back at my wisdom table.

NOTES

Who is currently sitting at your wisdom table that should no longer have a seat?

....

....

Who seems to want to resign?

....

....

....

....

9

Engaging Your Advisers

The last thing I want to share about your wisdom table is how you should engage those you desire to be a part of it. Make a list of all the people you can think of whose wisdom could shape your future. Again, think about the various categories in your life that are important to you. Remember, no one is likely to have all the wisdom you need in every area, so put together the right kind of board to cover the diverse areas in your life. Let me encourage you to start with five names. Here's the question that can help you determine your list:

> Out of everyone I know of right now, who do I most believe could bring the specific wisdom I need for my life?

Once you've made your list, there are some practical things to keep in mind as you pursue your wisdom table. While *who* you're seeking matters, it matters just as much *how* you seek to build your table. Here are some things I encourage you to keep in mind as you begin this process.

Don't ask for too much . . . in the beginning. Often, in our eagerness to get this right, we initially ask other people for way too much. Before you ask someone to sit at your wisdom table for the foreseeable future, just ask for an initial meeting. I encourage you to do this for a couple reasons. For starters, someone is way more likely to agree to meet with you once than to sign on for an indefinite period of time. Also, it gives the two of you a chance to get to know each other without putting pressure on either of you for a greater commitment. If the person is willing to meet with you, do it at a time that works for them—even if you have to move some things around in your own schedule.

When you have this first meeting, always go in prepared. Let the person know specifically what you'd like to talk to them about, or even beforehand you can send them a few questions you'd like to ask during your time together. I think it's wise to come with a journal or notebook as well as something to write with. I personally don't think it's helpful to use your phone to take notes on when you're having this kind of meeting.

Be respectful of the other person's time. Offer to pay for their meal or coffee. If the meeting seems to be going well, it's more than okay to ask questions about subsequent meetings. If you feel like this person would be a great addition to your wisdom table, let them know that. You might say something like, "I want to be a person who lives out God's purpose for my life. I know it's going to take a lot of wisdom to be able to do that, and I believe you could really help me. Would you be willing to meet with me like this every month or so?" If they are willing to be a source of wisdom in your life, congratulations! If they want to help but can't meet as frequently as monthly, that's okay. Just ask them if it's okay if you reach out to them when an opportunity or a crisis comes into your life. This lets them know you will only engage them when you really need something.

Sometimes you will discover there's no reason to have subsequent meetings. I have gone into some of these initial meetings with high hopes the person would be willing to be a mentor or coach. But during the meeting, I realized I might not gain any helpful wisdom by spending more time with them. It doesn't necessarily mean there's something wrong with this person. It just means when it comes to the specifics of what I'm navigating in my own life, they don't seem positioned to provide the needed wisdom.

Give them the upper hand. I am very particular about the kind of schedule I try to keep. I have found being vigilant with my calendar leads me to producing the best work God has called me to create and to fully living out the purposes he has given me in this season. That being said, I don't stick to my calendar when it comes to asking people to sit at my wisdom table. Because I value the wisdom and help someone can give me for my life, I am more than willing to alter my plans. For instance, I typically restrict every work morning to content creation. But if someone at my wisdom table is available to meet or call me only during this time, I'm happy to move other work around. In addition, I'm willing to go to their office, their home, or whatever location is convenient for them. This does not mean these individuals are more important to me than anything else in my life. I just happen to believe true wisdom is priceless.

Always be prepared. I mentioned doing this during your initial meetings, but you should be prepared every time you are with someone at your wisdom table. Spend time thinking and praying about the time you will spend with this person. Write down the most important questions you want to ask them. I think it's most helpful to them when you send these questions ahead of time. Make sure you are clear with the details of the meeting: where, when, and how long. Before leaving the meeting, make a clear ask about the next time the two of you can get together. The advisers you want to meet with already have plenty going on in their lives. Why would they be willing to prioritize their time with you? Because they see you've really thought about things before you share with them. They also want to know they are using their time to make an impact on others. When they can see the difference their wisdom is making in your life, it will be incredibly gratifying to them.

Give them your undivided attention. Whenever you are meeting with an adviser who sits at your wisdom table, it should be as though nothing else in the world is going on. You aren't trying to check your phone. You aren't focused on other people in the room. You aren't consumed with thinking of the next question you're going to ask them. You aren't trying to impress them with how much you know. (In fact, the less talking you do, the more wisdom you will gain.) You aren't thinking about the place you're headed once this meeting is over. You are giving your full attention to everything the person is saying. As John Mark Comer wrote, "What you give your attention to is the person you become."[1]

Don't hold back. If you have the right advisers at your wisdom table, they are going to be willing to tell you the truth. I want you to see this as their gift to you.

Let me share a temptation you will experience when it comes to meeting with individuals from your wisdom table. If something isn't going so well in your life, a part of you won't want to share that with them. You are worried about what they might think of you, how they will respond, or what they will ask you to do before the next time they meet with you. Tell them anyway! No one expects you to be perfect, but everyone at your wisdom table will expect you to be honest. Let them know which areas you are struggling in, and even the times you've blown it in a major way. If they care about you, they will be both firm and loving. And these are the exact kinds of people you want influencing your life. I bet they might even be willing to share some of their own past mistakes and what they learned from those experiences.

Have a meeting rhythm. It's helpful to have some regular rhythm of engaging with those at your wisdom table. It's likely your advisers lead busy lives just like you do. But it's also likely when something gets on their calendar, they stick to it. I think it's perfectly normal to ask someone, "What is a reasonable frequency for us to meet?" If nothing else, make sure you leave each meeting knowing when the next one will take place.

When it comes to my own wisdom table, I have people there who aren't able or willing to meet as often as I would like. I still want them to have a seat in my life. I'd much rather get wisdom from someone who can meet only once every ninety days than miss out on crucial wisdom that can impact my life.

Ask for access, but don't abuse that access. In addition to having a cadence for meeting face-to-face, it's also important to know if your advisers will give you access to communicating with them outside of these scheduled meetings. Hopefully they are willing to give you their phone number and email. If so, it's up to you to never abuse that access. Don't reach out to them flippantly or without thinking first about whether you really need to contact them.

When something comes up that causes me to need the input of my advisers, I reach out to them by text or email, letting them know I need to ask them something. I try to let them know what I need to discuss. Sometimes they can answer easily by text or email. Other times they tell me when they can talk by phone.

Find ways to bless those who serve at your wisdom table. Is there any way you can think of to serve the advisers at your wisdom table? Though you're coming to them for their wisdom, it's likely true there's something they could receive from you. Maybe they aren't tech savvy and you could help them with their computer issue or social media platform. Maybe they have a teenage son or daughter and you could serve them by investing in that teenager. Perhaps they love baseball and you just so happen to have tickets to an upcoming game (go Giants!). As you get to know them more, look for what God has given you that you could use to serve them.

I hope this concept of the wisdom table becomes a common language and practice in your life. As you can probably tell, I believe so much that our lives will be determined by what we do with these ideas and principles.

Even if you have assembled the ideal wisdom table for your life, there are still things that tend to get in the way. Let's examine what some of them are and see how we can overcome these obstacles.

NOTES

Out of everyone you know of right now, who do you most believe could bring the specific wisdom you need for your life?

SECTION THREE

What Is Stopping You?

There are obstacles to overcome so your vision becomes your reality.

10

The Great Paralyzer

You have now begun to understand something about your God-given purpose. You have started to build the ideal wisdom table for your current season of life. It is possible to know everything you can know. You can be confident of what God is calling you to step into. You can have the necessary financial resources. You can have the skills and abilities needed to do what God is calling you to do. All of this can be present, yet you still might find yourself completely paralyzed and unable to move forward. One thing all by itself could cause you to forfeit what God has for your future.

Fear is the great paralyzer for so many people. I see those who have so much going for them. They have strong dreams and compelling goals. They are part of a great church community where they are inspired on a weekly basis. They experience promptings from God, as though he is speaking directly to them. They have strong friendships with people who influence them for the good. But for some reason, fear continues to win the day in their hearts and in their lives.

You might recognize Hebrews 11 as the great chapter on faith in the Bible. But I think the last verse in chapter 10 sets the stage for everything we read in the chapter on faith. "We do not belong to those who shrink back and are destroyed, but to those who have faith and are saved" (v. 39). So much about your future is going to be determined by which of these two groups you choose to join. And I personally don't know anything that causes good people to shrink back more than fear. Think about this question:

What would you be attempting in your life if you weren't afraid?

What dreams would you pursue? What would you learn how to do for the first time? Who would you reach out to in hopes of having a friendship or relationship with them? What would you allow your children to do? Where would you travel? What promotion would you seek at work? What would you give yourself to because you're convinced you heard God speak directly to you about an initiative?

I have spent too much of my life being paralyzed by fear, and I'm guessing I'm not alone. I haven't been able to remove all my fears, but I have learned a few things that keep fear from paralyzing me any longer. And I'm passionate about seeing you freed from its jaws. There is so much that hangs in the balance for you and many others. Besides, what good is it to have a God-given purpose if fear keeps you from ever stepping into it?

The God who gives us our purpose is the same God telling us we don't have to be afraid.

Fear is natural and can even be healthy for us. There are things we should be afraid of, no doubt. But in the Bible, God always seems to be telling us to quit fearing the things he doesn't think we should be afraid of. Why are we told not to be afraid over 360 times throughout Scripture? Because God knows at least two things. First, he knows our natural inclination is to be afraid when we find ourselves in a challenging situation. And second, he knows fear will literally paralyze us and keep us from the life of faith he wants for us. Fear keeps us from becoming who God created us to be and from doing what he created us to do. It has caused countless numbers of people throughout history to miss out on what God had for them.

What if we don't have to miss out? What if we could begin to believe there is something—or rather, someone—who is stronger than all we're afraid of?

Psalm 27:1 says, "The LORD is my light and my salvation—whom shall I fear? The LORD is the stronghold of my life—of whom shall I be afraid?" Maybe overcoming our fear is more about God being with us than about us telling ourselves to quit being afraid. This correlation between God being present and fear being absent shows up all throughout the Bible. And in the book of Romans, Paul writes, "What, then, shall we say in response to these things? If God is for us, who can be against us?" (8:31). Perhaps we need to ask ourselves this question:

Do I really believe God is for me?

I wonder if growing our faith in this one belief could take care of so many of our fear issues.

I remember growing up with a strong sense that everyone was against me. I wish I could tell you why I believed this for much of my life. The only clarity I have looking back on my life is it was a completely irrational fear. This outlook caused me to assume God might be against me as well. So for much of my life, rather than thinking God was for me, I found myself afraid of God and what he might do to me.

Here's what I know for all of us: Until we believe God is for us, fear will remain a constant companion throughout our lives.

The difference between fear and faith has everything to do with what we see. In the book of Hebrews, we read, "Now faith is confidence in what we hope for and assurance about what we do not see" (11:1). If we are going to step away from a life of fear and step into a life of faith, we need a new set of eyes.

Are you able to see what you cannot see yet? To have vision for your life, it is crucial to be able to "see" what you cannot yet see with your physical eyes. Later in that same chapter in Hebrews, we read this about Moses: "By faith he left Egypt, not fearing the king's anger; he persevered because he saw him who is invisible" (v. 27). How in the world did Moses overcome his fears so that he was able to move forward in faith?

When God gives Moses his assignment of going to Pharaoh, Moses asks the first question all of us are prone to ask when God tells us he wants us to do something that seems impossible. "Who am I?" (Exod. 3:11). When God calls us into something that seems beyond what we think is possible for our lives, we automatically begin to look at our abilities and experiences. We're essentially asking ourselves, "Do I have what it takes?"

I find it quite interesting Moses is asking God to tell Moses who he is. But notice the answer from God. Or should I say, notice the lack of answer to Moses's question. Do you ever have people in your life who refuse to directly answer the question you are asking? This is exactly the kind of move God pulls with Moses. The first words out of his mouth are "I will be with you" (v. 12).

We want to know why God thinks we can pull something off. We want to look at our résumé and see if we have the necessary experience to move forward. We can't believe God thinks we can do it. And yet, God seems to think his presence with us will be enough.

Moses could have been paralyzed by fear when he looked around him. Everyone in Egypt knew there was no power like the power of Pharaoh. Moses was not known as an eloquent communicator, and he had spent the previous forty years as a shepherd in Midian. Let's be honest, this doesn't seem like the best career plan if you are preparing to go to the most powerful ruler in the known world. How did Moses not completely freak out when it was time to approach Pharaoh? Again, he "persevered because he saw him who is invisible" (Heb. 11:27). I love the play on words here. Moses was able to move into what God was calling him to do because he was able to see more than just what his earthly eyes captured.

It seems counterintuitive, but we must train ourselves to see more than simply what our physical eyes can see. Paul said it this way in his second letter to the Corinthian church: "So we fix our eyes not on what is seen, but on what is unseen, since what is seen is temporary, but what is unseen is eternal" (2 Cor. 4:18). If all we can see is all there is, we should probably be afraid. But if we can have eyes of faith in the God who is ever-present, we can move forward in faith.

Fear causes us to be focused on the obstacle, while faith in God causes us to be focused on the opportunity.

While everyone thought they knew Pharaoh to be the most powerful authority on the planet, God wanted to introduce a higher power, and he did this through the life of Moses. Imagine what God might want to display through you. You might think you're just a stay-at-home mom or just a college student or just a bank teller, but God sees way more than just what you see. After all, he is the God who took Moses from leading sheep for four decades straight into freeing two million slaves in Egypt.

Because Moses was able to approach Pharaoh, God delivered the Israelites after four hundred years of slavery. As you think about this, what is at stake in your own life? What purpose is God wanting to accomplish in and through you? What happens if fear continues to win the day?

What if fear had paralyzed Moses when God gave him his purpose? Moses got the faith versus fear thing right, at least in this instance. I want to introduce you to some others who, for whatever reason, were unable to train their eyes to see what God wanted to give them. The best way to get a full overview of this story is to read Numbers 13–14. This is where the action takes place, but there are many references in the Bible that point back to this historic moment. It's that profound.

When God comes to free the Israelites in Egypt, he isn't only wanting to take them out of a bad situation. When God calls us out of something, he is also wanting to call us into something. So he brings the Israelites out of Egypt with the full intention of bringing them into Canaan, also known as the promised land. God tells Moses to send twelve leaders to explore the land. But notice what else he says to Moses: "Send some men to explore the land of Canaan, *which I am giving to the Israelites*" (Num. 13:2, emphasis added). These spies explore this land and are gone for forty days. They come back and report what they have discovered. "They gave Moses this account: 'We went into the land to which you sent us, and it does flow with milk and honey! Here is its fruit. But the people who live there are powerful, and the cities are fortified and very large. We even saw descendants of Anak there'" (vv. 27–28). In other words, the land is amazing, but there are some major obstacles.

Anytime God has something for us to do in the world, we will find opportunities and obstacles present. And it really matters which one we tend to focus on more. It's not about pretending obstacles don't exist. We just need to decide which we are going to magnify—God's promise or the challenges between us and the fulfillment of that promise.

Caleb, one of the twelve who explored the land, silences the people and says, "We should go up and take possession of the land, for we can certainly do it" (v. 30). It would make for a great movie if the other eleven responded by saying, "Caleb, you're absolutely right. Let's go for it!" Unfortunately, the response he receives is quite the opposite. Most of the others claim they are unable to take the land because the people living there are stronger than them. Remember what we read earlier about this land. God is *giving* it to the Israelites.

Often God wants to give us something, but we are unwilling to take possession of it.

What are the things God wants to give you but you are unwilling to step into because you fear everything that stands between you and what he is offering? What opportunities have you been unable to seize, simply out of fear? We have given more power to the obstacles in our lives than to the God who claims to have all authority in heaven and on earth.

Fear distorts how we see God's intentions for our lives. The Israelites begin to believe God brought them out of Egypt only to kill them in the desert. They actually believe God is taking them somewhere so he can kill them. But the reality is, he is taking them somewhere new so he can give them life, not death.

I'll never forget the day a retired minister came to see me. He came to my office at the church I previously worked in. At the time of his visit, everyone knew we felt like God was calling us to move to San Francisco and start a new church. He said to me, "You know why God put the San Andreas fault line out there near San Francisco, don't you?" I was thinking, *No, but I'm sure you're going to tell me.* He went on to say it was because of God's judgment, and then he said, "If you go out there, you're going to be there when the next big one [an earthquake] comes." Now, how would you have responded? He might have been right; it's no secret the San Francisco Bay Area is more prone to earthquakes than other places. That meeting certainly left me with something to think about.

As I'm writing this chapter, it's been right at fifteen years since that meeting. What would I have missed out on these past fifteen years if fear had won me over? What would my kids have missed out on? What would our Epic Church community have missed out on? What would our local and global partners be missing out on right now if we hadn't come in spite of the obstacles? We've spent enough of our lives trying to go back to Egypt, back to what is so familiar, even if it's nowhere close to God's intended destination for our lives.

What might you miss out on for the next fifteen years if fear keeps winning in your life?

Thankfully two of the Israelite leaders are able to see more than just the obstacles. Caleb and Joshua say to the group, "Do not rebel against the LORD. And do not be afraid of the people of the land, because we will devour them. Their protection is gone, but the LORD is with us. Do not be afraid of them" (Num. 14:9).

We want God to protect us from difficult circumstances. But what we should want is for God to protect us from anything that will derail us from his purpose for our lives. What if, instead of being people paralyzed by our fears, we could constantly be galvanized by our faith?

These leaders in Israel were so paralyzed by their fears, they refused to believe the God who had already freed them from Pharaoh. "The LORD said to Moses, 'How long will these people treat me with contempt? How long will they refuse to believe in me, in spite of all the signs I have performed among them?'" (v. 11). Sometimes I wonder, *How many times does*

God have to show up and act in our lives before we're willing to believe him for whatever he calls us to in the future?

What have you seen God do previously in your life? In spite of his past activity, are you still doubting he will provide what's needed in your current season? Think about where he has taken you so far. Make a list of the ways he has provided for you. May we not be people whom God has to ask, "How long will you refuse to believe in me, in spite of everything I have already done for you?"

Before we close this chapter, it's important you know your battle with fear will likely continue to resurface throughout your life. It still shows up at various times in my own life. When the COVID-19 pandemic began in early March of 2020, it brought a paralyzing fear to the whole world. *Will I get this virus? How deadly is it going to be? Will it affect people I know and love? Will I be able to keep my job? How long will our children miss attending school in person?*

That season was the most difficult one I have had as a leader. Our church couldn't hold normal Sunday gatherings for sixty-eight weeks. Many people were moving away from San Francisco. I didn't know what our financial reality would be, so I was afraid of having to lay off staff members. I didn't know what our church would look like when this long season was over. People left our church, and others completely walked away from their faith.

Leading during this tumultuous time had a profound effect on me. In March 2021, I felt completely depleted and made plans to take a solitude retreat. I reserved a hotel in Napa Valley for a couple of nights. I spent my time resting, reflecting, and trying to make sense of what had happened over the previous twelve months. Here is some of what I wrote during that time:

This past year has been filled with so much challenge and pressure. Leading a family with kids who haven't stepped foot in their classrooms in over a year. Leading a church who has gone over a year without having a normal Sunday gathering. Fear has to go. And so does anxiety. I was afraid that our giving would go down, but that hasn't been the case. I thought we might have to lay off staff members, but that conversation hasn't come anywhere near reality. So many people in our Epic community with so many needs throughout this past year—spiritual, financial, emotional, mental, relational, and physical. We called. We served. We gave.

So much of this past year has just been every day feeling like the same, but my personality has usually thrived off bringing special experiences to Shauna, our kids, our team, and our church. But the options have been so incredibly limited. At various times, I've become too addicted to compulsively checking the news for signs of hope. It's robbed me of peace and of being present to God and the people in my life. It has also kept me from being fully focused on the good work God prepared for me to do— even in a tumultuous season.

Below is my summary statement for all I learned during this season. I pray you can adopt it for whatever scary things come your way in the future:

Things can get way worse than you fear, but you are in better hands than you think.

Let God's past activity in your life fuel your faith in his future activity.

NOTES

What would you be attempting in your life if you weren't afraid?

Do you really believe God is for you?

What might you miss out on for the next fifteen years if fear keeps winning in your life?

11

Leaving the Familiar

How much do you enjoy change in your life? I tend to like the idea of doing something new, but facing the reality of change can be so daunting for me. I don't know about you, but I find a great deal of comfort in the people, things, and places that are familiar. Unfortunately, familiarity can be one of the things that holds us back the most. It can keep us from moving forward, even when we know it's time for a new chapter in our story.

To step into what God has for you, you will often need to walk away from something that's become familiar to you.

Think about your favorite stories from the Bible. We love seeing people or groups take new ground in some way. We love to hear about what God did for someone in the face of impossibility. When he called that person or group to step into something new he had for them, did they have to leave something familiar? Moses had to leave the familiarity of shepherding before he could ever go to Pharaoh and free the nation of Israel. Nehemiah had to leave the familiarity of his job as cupbearer to the king before he could ever go back and rebuild Jerusalem. Esther had to be willing to leave the mindset that she was just in the palace to be the queen if she was ever going to step up and save her people. Listen in on what Luke tells us the disciples had to leave in order to follow Jesus: "They pulled their boats up on shore, left everything and followed him" (Luke 5:11).

It seems clear leaving what's familiar isn't an exception when it comes to stepping into what God has for us. This is the normal pattern for all of us who want to move toward the story God is wanting to write with our lives. Consider Jesus himself. He's always existed. He's always been in the presence of God the Father. But for him to carry out the mission of his life, he had to leave the familiarity of heaven and step into the unfamiliar territory of a human body—a tiny one at that. Do not think you will be able to accomplish the mission God has for your life unless you first step away from what he no longer has for you.

When the idea of starting a new church first entered my mind, I was thirty-one years old. I was serving as a teaching pastor at a large church in the Midwest. I had been hired to teach weekly for one of our Sunday services. The senior pastor was fifty-six at the time, and we hit it off right away. He became a great mentor to me, and I knew he could help in my development. I assumed I'd be in this role for many years, and I intended to make the most of it. This was an amazing setup for me and for our family. I had a great work-life balance during this season, which was helpful as our three sons were all under the age of five. I had just been accepted into a doctorate program focused on preaching and leadership. Our closest friends lived two houses down from us. Everything was present for the kind of life we had sought to live, and then came the calling of starting a church in a city far from where our ideal life had been created.

If we were going to move to San Francisco to start a new church, we would have to walk away from all kinds of familiarity.

We would have to leave a familiar church for one that didn't even exist yet. We would have to leave our close friends and go make new ones. I had never been a lead pastor before, which meant there was always someone above me to provide protection and coverage. Raising our kids in a major city like San Francisco meant we would have to leave the familiarity of the safe and high-caliber school system we thought our kids would always attend. I had to leave the familiarity of having a guaranteed paycheck and venture into a fundraising world where nothing was promised. Our family would have to walk away from a familiar culture to step into a culture that was as different as you can imagine.

I knew Shauna and I had to be honest with ourselves about what we would be giving up and walking away from. Not knowing how best to do this, I simply got out a sheet of yellow notebook paper and made two columns. The first column included things we would willingly walk away from, while the second column involved things we would never give up. We wrote down a number of things we would give up to step into what God had for us. Here are a few of them: ever owning a home again, comfortable schools for our kids, the size of our home, and living close to our families. We wrote only two things in the second column: a thriving marriage and our kids being able to do well in San Francisco. This exercise helped us so much, and I still have this commitment to our family today.

There are some familiar things you should never walk away from. At the same time, there will be many familiar things you will have to walk away from.

What is familiar to you that you can't even imagine having to walk away from?

Maybe you can't imagine walking away from your job or at least the industry you've been working in for a number of years. Perhaps you're in a dating relationship you can't imagine walking away from. It could be you've lived in your city or town for a number of years, and you could never see yourself moving away. It could even be you simply have a habit that is so familiar, you wouldn't recognize your life without it. I'm not suggesting God is necessarily asking you to leave any of these things. But what if he did? What if he has something different, even better, for you?

I have noticed a pattern recently, simply by paying attention to what my friends are experiencing in their lives. Sometimes God has to take something away from us before we can ever receive the new thing he wants to do in our lives.

I have a very close friend who served as the right-hand person to the CEO of a technology start-up in Silicon Valley. They had a great relationship, and the CEO had the utmost trust in my friend. Eventually their company was acquired by a major corporation. Because so many people in our church work in this space, I've come to learn acquisitions usually mean things change in a major way. Under pressure from the new company's leadership, the CEO let my friend go from his position. As you can imagine, this crushed him. It upset and confused him and left him wondering if he had what it takes to be successful. Since then, he has been able to consult with multiple start-up companies. This is just my opinion, but I think it's right: God had to get him out of one job before he could step into these other opportunities.

Another friend of mine had a neighbor who set out to make his family's life miserable. It got so bad my friend and his family couldn't stay in that home. As you might imagine, this was frustrating. But now they have an amazing home in an even better location. They never would have asked for less-than-ideal neighbors, but those challenging neighbors had a part to play in opening up a new blessing from God.

God might have to take something away from you to position you to receive something that is even better.

When it comes to stories about leaving the familiar, I think we can learn a lot from Abraham. I love the following brief summary of how he lived out his faith. The book of Hebrews says this about him:

> By faith Abraham, when called to go to a place he would later receive as his inheritance, obeyed and went, even though he did not know where he was going. By faith he made his home in the promised land like a stranger in a foreign country; he lived in tents, as did Isaac and Jacob, who were heirs with him of the same promise. For he was looking forward to the city with foundations, whose architect and builder is God. (11:8–10)

Sometimes God calls us to leave one thing before he tells us exactly what's coming next. This was the case for Abraham. It's hard enough for us to leave the familiar when we know what's ahead. How could he leave when he didn't even know where he was going? I think he was able to do this because he became convinced of something we must become convinced of: *Knowing "who" is even more important than knowing "what."* Because Abraham was looking forward, he was able to walk away from what was behind him.

I feel like so many of us are unable to walk into what's ahead of us because we're so focused on what's behind us. There's nothing wrong with looking back over where we've been in life and reflecting on that. Looking back can give us amazing reminders of God's power, presence, faithfulness, and provision. And looking back in this way can provide the fuel we need to trust God for what's next. But there's another thing that looking back can lead to. It can cause us to long to go back to where we were. We can long for a previous season or a previous job or a previous place we called home. This kind of looking back causes us to crave familiarity as though that must be what's best for us.

It seems counterproductive to ask God to bless where we are if he has already told us to leave that place.

Abraham could choose to build a life for himself or step into what God wanted to build through his life. You have the exact same choice. I know leaving the familiar is challenging. You probably already have ideas about the kind of life you want to build. But before you cling to what's so familiar, let me encourage you to let go of what has been so you can live into what could be.

We are going to have to walk away from one thing or another. There's a temptation for us to want to have it all, do it all, and be it all. But that isn't possible. Every one of us will make sacrifices for the rest of our lives. We will set down one thing in order to have something else.

Do you want to walk away from what has been in the past or from what could be in the future?

Leaving the familiar doesn't always mean a new city or a new job or a new whatever. Shauna and I have experienced many different seasons in our marriage, even though we've been married to the same person for over two decades. We are still parents to the same four kids who are quite familiar to us. However, each new parenting stage has required us to leave some familiar things and step into brand-new realities. I have already worked for Epic Church four times as long as I've worked for any other organization. Though my position has been the same since the founding of our church, each season has required me to let go of some things so I could pick up others.

Leaving the familiar is challenging, even when we step into something far better than what we're leaving behind. After spending this chapter urging you to leave what's familiar, I want to encourage you to learn how to grieve endings well. Go ahead and say goodbye. Cry it out. Write a thank-you note to God and the people who have been a part of this season that's coming to a close. Grieve and then step out. The future God has for you will only be found on the other side of you walking away from something that's familiar.

NOTES

What is familiar to you that you can't even imagine having to walk away from?

Do you want to walk away from what has been in the past or from what could be in the future?

12

Missing What Matters Most

There is more coming into our lives than ever before. There is more information available to us than we've ever had access to. We are now able to be connected, at least virtually, to more people than ever before. There are more television channels, more sources of news, and more entertainment options than we've ever had in the history of our world.

All of this might be okay if we had unlimited time, unlimited money, unlimited energy, and unlimited capacity. But we don't. And because we don't, there is something that tends to keep us from the life we want and the life God wants for us. We are distracted. And I don't simply mean we aren't focused enough. I mean we are so distracted we are missing what matters most. And we're so busy we rarely stop to consider all the things we're missing out on. There has to be a better way.

> What are the distractions that have the power to pull you away from the things you could be giving your life to?

There's so much noise everywhere. We hear so many voices every single day. Voices asking us to prove ourselves. Voices telling us what we must have to be happy. Voices condemning us for what we did five years ago. Voices telling us we don't have enough—enough money, enough status, or enough experience. What if we are so distracted by all the voices around us, we are missing the voice that matters most?

Though he didn't live in the digital age, Jesus also heard a lot of noise throughout his life. He encountered so many voices—voices telling him to be a different kind of Messiah, voices telling him to prove himself, voices telling him he was crazy, and even voices claiming he must be possessed by demons. And these voices came from all over the place—religious leaders, political leaders, the devil, his disciples, and even his own family. So how did he keep from being distracted? How did he continue to focus on the voice that mattered most? And is there anything we can learn from how he did this?

When Jesus was baptized, he heard a voice that would be the defining voice over his entire life. "A voice from heaven said, 'This is my Son, whom I love; with him I am well pleased'" (Matt. 3:17). I don't think he ever forgot that voice. I believe this was a moment Jesus constantly went back to, a moment that kept him anchored in his purpose for the rest of his earthly life.

When he was tempted to believe something else was true, when groups of people started challenging him about who he really was, when he felt all alone, I imagine he would replay those words in his heart and mind over and over. To tune in to the voice of God, he had to ignore many other voices.

If we are going to tune in to the voice of God, we will have to ignore many other voices in this world.

Just after hearing this pronouncement from his heavenly Father, Jesus is led into the wilderness to be tempted by the devil for forty days. Matthew gives us three specific temptations, but I believe all three of them can be summarized in one overarching temptation Jesus faced and we face:

Our greatest temptation is to forget the voice of God.

When Jesus is in the wilderness, the devil tries to entice him to no longer focus on his Father's voice. He challenges Jesus to prove himself if he really is the Son of God.

I'm sure you're familiar with the voices that challenge you to prove yourself. They come from outside of you and inside of you. Here are how some of my temptations to prove myself go: *Ben, if you're really a great husband, then wouldn't you be more _____? Ben, if you were the kind of dad your kids need, wouldn't you be a little more _____? Ben, if you are going to be the kind of leader to bring Epic Church into the future, don't you think you ought to be a little better at _____?*

This is exactly what we see with the first temptation mentioned in the Bible. God tells Adam and Eve to enjoy the fruit from all the trees except one. The serpent asks them, "Did God really say, 'You must not eat from any tree in the garden'?" (Gen. 3:1). He is doing everything he can to get them to distrust God's voice.

I see this happening throughout our world today, and I'm guessing you aren't immune to it. What voices are trying to distract you from hearing and following God's voice for your life? You might think, from the above example, that only the voice of the devil is trying to do this. I wish you were right about that, but his voice isn't the only one trying to take you away from what God has for you.

Peter was one of the twelve disciples of Jesus, and he was distinguished even within that group of men. He, along with James and John, formed the inner circle with Jesus. They got invited into spaces the other nine did not. They were asked to pray for Jesus during his darkest hour. Peter was passionate about following Jesus, but only on his own terms.

There came a time when Jesus began telling his disciples he must suffer many things and ultimately be killed by the religious leaders. This didn't fit into the plan Peter had for Jesus. "Peter took him aside and began to rebuke him. 'Never, Lord!' he said. 'This shall never happen to you.' Jesus turned and said to Peter, 'Get behind me, Satan! You are a stumbling block to me; you do not have in mind the concerns of God, but merely human concerns'" (Matt. 16:22–23). Peter was one of the closest people to Jesus, and even he was trying to distract Jesus from the mission he was meant to give his life for.

It's challenging when a friend distracts us from our mission. It can be even more painful, however, when the distraction comes from a family member.

One day there was a large crowd gathering to be near Jesus, and his family got news he was causing a commotion. "When his family heard about this, they went to take charge of him, for they said, 'He is out of his mind'" (Mark 3:21). Though I wish this wasn't the case, sometimes you'll have to choose to listen to the voice of God over the voice of your own family.

Is there any person or group tempting you to live out of the image they have created for you?

There isn't enough time to give significant attention to things that just aren't significant. It seems like all of us wish we had more time. We think if we did, we wouldn't be so busy. Or we would get more rest. Or we would enjoy more time with the people we say mean the most to us. But are those really the things we would do if we had more time? If there was an eighth day added to your week, what do you think you would do with the extra twenty-four hours?

Do you think God got it wrong when it comes to time allocation? I mean, maybe twenty-four hours were enough for a day back when there was no electricity, there was no major travel, and you didn't know as many people. Or perhaps God knew exactly what he was doing in giving us twenty-four hours a day.

I know most of us are busy. I know most of us already know how to fill or even overfill our time. I also know we can struggle with the idea of having limited time. But what if we aren't giving our time to what matters most? What if, instead, we are distracted by all the things that don't matter most?

I love this prayer from Moses: "Teach us to number our days, that we may gain a heart of wisdom" (Ps. 90:12). If you're constantly busy, exhausted, and overwhelmed, could it be possible you're trying to give your time to things God never intended for you to give your time to? J. Oswald Sanders, who directed a global missions effort for decades, said, "Each of us has the time to do the whole will of God for our lives."[1]

You and I have the time to do absolutely everything God has assigned to our lives. You know what we don't have time to do? The things God isn't asking us to do with our lives. Sanders went on to say, "Often the pressure a spiritual leader feels comes from assuming tasks that God has not assigned; for such tasks the leader cannot expect God to supply the extra strength required."[2]

My aim for writing this book is to help you get locked in on what God has for your life in this current season. Here's a by-product of really focusing in on that: It will keep you from becoming distracted by all the stuff God does not have for you.

There are things we were meant to give our time to in one season that we no longer need to give our time to. Our focus in an earlier season can become a distraction in a different season.

When we were in the season of starting Epic Church, there were so many things that required a wise use of my time. I made sure I knew every detail about every single area of our church: what curriculum our kids' ministry was using and what each member of our staff was doing on a daily basis. Those things made sense at the time. Now we are in a different season and there are other things that deserve my time. I must spend a certain amount of time investing in our growing staff, but I don't need to know everything they're doing every single day. I can no longer be focused on just the next few months; I must be thinking about what's ahead for the next few years.

> **What are you still trying to give your attention to that is distracting you from what could be present in your current season?**

The Bible seems to indicate two things about time: It is short, and it is sufficient. Time is limited, but there is enough of it to live the life God is calling you to live.

One of the most amazing things about the humanity of Jesus is it meant he limited himself to twenty-four hours a day. I love this insight from Sanders: "Conscious of time, Jesus spent His time doing things that mattered."[3] What if Jesus had gotten distracted? What if he hadn't given his time to what mattered most? What would we have missed out on?

I know we're talking about Jesus here, but I think the same criteria applies to you and me. What happens if we get distracted? What if we don't make the contribution God sent us into this world to make? Who all is going to miss out if we don't stay focused on what God has for us?

You might think the distraction temptations lessen as you grow throughout your life. I wish that was true, but unfortunately the opposite is true. The more success and growth take place in your life, the more two things are going to increase for you: potential opportunities and potential relationships. It sounds counterintuitive, but the more you stay focused on what you're supposed to do, the more opportunities will come for you to be distracted.

As you think about how this applies to your life, let me share how it has applied to mine. Because I stayed focused on starting Epic Church, it got off the ground. Because we got a church off the ground in San Francisco, that piqued the interest of other people. This meant they wanted to meet with me so they could hear about what had happened. And just like that, I had more people asking for my time in that season than in a previous season.

When our family moved to San Francisco, we hardly knew anyone living here. More than a decade later, that is no longer the case. Our kids have now gone to multiple schools. They have played on quite a few sports teams. Our church has also grown during this time. All of this is great, but it also means we now have way more people asking for our time, though we still have only the same twenty-four hours we started with.

One of the things I've had to learn in recent years is my number of yeses must stay the same or even decrease in every new season. Because the number of potential opportunities and potential relationships is only going to increase, I will have to say way more nos in every new season.

How comfortable are you saying no? If you're going to get in on all that God has for you, I suggest you get very comfortable with it. Once you gain clarity on what God's yeses are for you, this clarifies that almost everything else will be a no.

If I could give you advice on how to embrace this for your own life, here is what I'd tell you: Don't focus on what you're saying no to; instead, find the joy in what you're saying yes to in this season.

When Nehemiah is feeling compelled to go back and rebuild Jerusalem, his yes means he has to say no to being the king's cupbearer—at least for a season. But this isn't the only no he has to give. Nehemiah faces opposition in his attempt to rebuild

Jerusalem, and the goal of his opponents is simple: distraction. They try to take him away from what he's seeking to give his energy to. Nehemiah learns something you need to know:

There will always be people who want to say no to the yes God places over your life.

These opponents keep coming to Nehemiah. One time they ask him to come and meet with them. You and I might think that sounds quite reasonable, but that's not how Nehemiah interprets it. He sees it as a distraction. Nehemiah doesn't even go and tell them no himself. He sends messengers to tell them, "I am doing a great work and I cannot come down. Why should the work stop while I leave it and come down to you?" (Neh. 6:3 ESV).

What if this could become your go-to response every time you find yourself tempted to get distracted by what isn't the best use of your time in this season? "I am doing a great work and I cannot come down." This is such a good reminder that can help you stay focused on what God has for you. Whatever he has for you, it is a great work. Why should you stop that to give your attention to what someone else wants for you?

But know this—you won't have to say no only once. Nehemiah continues to hear from his opponents: "They sent to me four times in this way, and I answered them in the same manner" (v. 4 ESV). He has to keep saying no so he can keep saying his right yes.

Nehemiah completes the wall in only fifty-two days. How did this happen? He has God's favor on his life and this project. He also has an amazing team who goes after the vision with him. But there's one more reason he completes it so quickly. Nehemiah sees his vision become a reality because he refuses to be distracted by anything that isn't part of the vision. What could you accomplish if you could keep yourself from being distracted by everything that isn't a part of your God-given vision?

NOTES

What are the distractions that have the power to pull you away from the things you could be giving your life to?

_____

_____

_____

_____

Is there any person or group tempting you to live out of the image they have created for you?

_____

_____

_____

_____

What are you still trying to give your attention to that is distracting you from what could be present in your current season?

_____

_____

_____

_____

13

Where's Your Close Eye?

In the last chapter, we talked broadly about how distraction keeps us from stepping into the things we've been called to give our lives to. I want to spend this chapter focusing on the one distraction that is keeping so many of us from what we could be giving our time and energy to. I'm convinced this distraction has never been stronger in the history of the world. I'm also convinced if you consistently succumb to it, you will end up forfeiting the future God has for you. I'm talking about the distraction known as *comparison*.

It makes sense why this is stronger now than it's ever been throughout human history. We have more access to the lives of other people than we've ever had before. Thanks to social media, you no longer have to wonder how you stack up against every other person on the planet. You simply have to follow them and see what they have that you don't have, where they've been that you'll probably never go, and what they've accomplished that you can't even dream of doing.

It's not just social media, though. The game of comparison is everywhere. You can now compare your LinkedIn profile to everyone else's. You can compare how you're doing on exercise versus your friends or people you've never met. You can see on Goodreads how many books others have read in comparison to you. You can even have a "friend" on your Bible reading app and see if they've been skipping days while you've been faithful (even if only because you know they're watching).

The comparison trap can and will happen to all of us if we aren't careful. I can scroll Instagram and see how amazing every other church is in our city, in our nation, and even around the world. If I'm in a healthy place, I will thank God for those churches and the work they are doing. If I'm in an unhealthy place, I will feel inferior and think I don't measure up.

It's just as bad if we look at others and feel superior to them. Is it possible that as we've fixed our eyes on everyone else's life, we're missing out on the one life we should be focused on—the one God has for us? Please understand I'm not advocating for a self-absorbed life. In fact, there's no way to live the life God has called us to and make it all about ourselves. If we're going to bring out what God has put into us, it really matters what our eyes are fixed on.

Around 1000 BC, the leaders of Israel begin to ask the prophet Samuel for a king. They had never had a king before. God claims they had rejected him as their king and had requested a human king. He tells Samuel to anoint Saul as their new king. Over time, Saul gets to know David and becomes very fond of him. He makes David one of his armor-bearers. As you probably know, David goes on to kill Goliath. I want you to watch how quickly Saul's view of David begins to change. I think this is a profound case study on how comparison causes us to forfeit the life God has for us.

> Whatever mission Saul sent him on, David was so successful that Saul gave him a high rank in the army. This pleased all the troops, and Saul's officers as well.

When the men were returning home after David had killed the Philistine, the women came out from all the towns of Israel to meet King Saul with singing and dancing, with joyful songs and with timbrels and lyres. As they danced, they sang:

> "Saul has slain his thousands,
>   and David his tens of thousands."

Saul was very angry; this refrain displeased him greatly. "They have credited David with tens of thousands," he thought, "but me with only thousands. What more can he get but the kingdom?" And from that time on Saul kept a close eye on David. (1 Sam. 18:5–9)

How in the world did David go from being Saul's favorite to becoming the person Saul wanted to kill the most? He had done nothing different from when Saul thought he was the most amazing person ever. The difference that changed everything between these two—and, I would argue, that changed the rest of Saul's life—was Saul realizing he didn't quite stack up to David. He was good with David as long as he was above him. He even gave him a high ranking in the army, though David was still underneath him.

The women from all the towns come out to meet King Saul with singing and dancing. Notice they begin their song with this line: "Saul has slain his thousands." The whole point of their song, at least at this point, is to honor Saul. He must have felt good about himself and all he accomplished. The only problem for him is their song keeps going: ". . . and David his tens of thousands." Now Saul is no longer content with what he has done or how he is seen by others. He gets very angry, as this comparison displeases him greatly. The women have credited David with tens of thousands and Saul with only thousands.

By the way, you can never celebrate someone you are jealous of. Saul could have been grateful. He could have been amazed by remembering the lowly place he had come from and all God had done for him. But he was not because he was fixated on the comparison game with David.

> **When it comes to the comparison game, you lose even if you win.**

Here's the verse that tells you everything you need to know about how comparison really works: "And from that time on Saul kept a close eye on David" (v. 9). He is no longer content with what he's been given. He is no longer focusing his energies on what God has for his life. Saul becomes obsessed with David from here on out.

Comparison destroys what could be present in our lives because it causes us to keep our "close eye" on someone else. Let me ask you a question:

What are you keeping your close eye on?

There's nothing wrong with glancing at the lives of others. I think there are two primary reasons to do so: to cheer them on and to learn from them. But we cannot keep our close eye on someone else's life and stay focused on the life we're meant to live.

If you are a mom, cheer other moms on, but don't keep a close eye on their lives and whether they're doing better or worse than you are. If you are a church leader, pray and learn from other church leaders, but don't spend energy trying to figure out if you're better than them. When it comes to your job, a win for you is not winning against your coworkers. You do the best job you can with what's on your plate and let them do the same.

If we aren't supposed to keep a close eye on anyone else, what are we supposed to do with our eyes? The book of Hebrews has the answer:

Therefore, since we are surrounded by such a great cloud of witnesses, let us throw off everything that hinders and the sin that so easily entangles. And let us run with perseverance the race marked out for us, *fixing our eyes on Jesus*, the pioneer and perfecter of faith. For the joy set before him he endured the cross, scorning its shame, and sat down at the right hand of the throne of God. (12:1–2, emphasis added)

If we are called to throw off everything that hinders our lives, comparison has to be included in that. It keeps us from loving people well. It keeps us from being content with who God has made us to be and what he has called us to do. It doesn't allow us to give our time to the things that are most significant. We must run *the race marked out for us*.

God has graced your life with a specific purpose. You are called to run your race. Who cares if you win a race God has never called you to run?

I have several friends who run in long-distance races. They know there's no way they'll run a good race if they keep their eyes focused on how everyone else around them is running. The same is true when it comes to the race of our lives. And then we're given the example of Jesus. He didn't get sidetracked by what everyone else was doing. He stayed laser-focused on the life (and death) God had called him to run.

You will never run the race God has for you as long as you are consumed with the race he has for everyone else.

Comparison removes contentment. It channels your energy away from what matters most. It also causes a lack of gratitude toward the God who has given you so much.

John the Baptist shows us how to fight against the comparison trap we're tempted to fall into. Before Jesus had a public ministry, John was the one everyone was coming to. When Jesus comes onto the scene, John's disciples are like, "John, everyone is going to him." They begin comparing him and Jesus, afraid he might be losing out. I love John's response: "A person can receive only what is given them from heaven" (John 3:27). He refuses to play the comparison game. Why? I think he is content with what God has given him and with what God has not given him.

Can we get there? What if we began to be content with what God has given us as well as what he has not given us? This will help you and me to keep our close eye on God and what he has for us.

As we think about this concept of a close eye, here's a question to consider:

What does God keep his close eye on?

When God tells Samuel to anoint the next king after Saul, he says it will be one of Jesse's sons. When Samuel sees David's brother Eliab, he thinks he has found the future king. It's at this point God tells Samuel what he keeps a close eye on. "The LORD said to Samuel, 'Do not consider his appearance or his height, for I have rejected him. The LORD does not look at the things people look at. People look at the outward appearance, but the LORD looks at the heart'" (1 Sam. 16:7). God doesn't keep a close eye on what everyone else wants to compare. He sees through our appearances and the images we've created for ourselves. And he's never comparing you and me to anyone else. He's simply interested in whether or not we're doing what he has for us to do.

We miss out on what God has for us when we're so distracted by what God has for everyone else.

You may know Peter was the disciple who denied Jesus three times. After Jesus rises from the dead, he has a conversation with Peter to restore him. Jesus wraps up this conversation with Peter by telling him some familiar words: "Follow me!" (John 21:19). You would think this would be enough for Peter. You would think, after blowing it before, he would merely be grateful to do whatever Jesus wanted him to do with his life. But when Peter sees John, known as the disciple whom Jesus loved, he asks, "'Lord, what about him?' Jesus answered, 'If I want him to remain alive until I return, what is that to you? You must follow me'" (vv. 21–22). Before we start judging Peter, haven't we all done this before? Jesus tells us to follow him, and we get interested in what he has for everyone else. Why does that matter so much? We've all been given a different race to run.

Let me tell you when I have seen this show up in my own life. Sometimes I attach this question to everyone and everything around me: *What does this mean about me?* If someone is complimented, what does that mean about me? If someone is told they are a great leader, what does that mean about me? If someone praises another person on our staff, what does that mean about me? If I'm not thinking correctly, I will believe all these things mean I'm less than or not as significant as the person being praised. Here's the truth of what all these things mean about me: *absolutely nothing.*

What is present in someone else isn't at all about what is absent in you.

You cannot be whoever you want to be, but you can be whoever God is calling you to be. And contrary to popular thinking, you cannot do anything you want to do. However, you can do anything God is calling you to do. But you know what you can never do? Run your race while being consumed with everyone else's.

At the end of the day, God isn't going to ask you how you ran my race. And he isn't going to ask me how I ran yours. He's going to hold me accountable for the life he had for me, and he's going to hold you accountable for the life he called you to live.

God has a glorious life for you. Quit wishing you were someone else or had someone else's talents. There's only one you. What God desires and what the rest of this world needs is for you to do exactly what God has graced you to do.

NOTES

What are you keeping your close eye on?

What does God keep his close eye on?

14

Owning Your Part

If you're like me, there have probably been seasons of your life when you didn't take full responsibility for the things you were genuinely responsible for. Maybe you knew God had asked you to do some specific thing with your life, but for whatever reason, you never did it. Or maybe you were making choices that were negatively impacting your physical health. It could even be your team dropped the ball on a work project, but you refused to take responsibility for the part you played in it.

I wish I didn't have an abundance of examples for when I refused to own up to or take responsibility for certain things in my life. There's one experience from my teenage years that perfectly illustrates this. A family in our church was hosting a swim party and I wanted to go. The only problem was my car was parked in front of my mom's car. Unfortunately, she had not left the keys to her car. As a teenager who really wanted to go to the party, I wasn't going to let this fact deter me. I thought, *I'll just reverse my car at an angle to avoid contact with hers.* The good news? I avoided hitting her car. The bad news? While trying to avoid her car, I hit a red pole in our carport. And there was red paint all over my gray car. Rather than own up to it, I thought I would just figure out a way to fix it.

I drove to the store in search of gray spray paint (yes, I've always been a genius). The store was out of gray, but they did have black. Don't judge me; desperate times call for desperate measures. I bought the black spray paint and covered the red paint on my car. It was dark outside by then, and from everything I could see, it looked like I had done the job. I went to the swim party and had a good time.

The next morning, I was woken up by the sound of my dad's voice. "Benjamin, come here" was all he said. I knew this wouldn't be a good start to my day. My dad asked me to go outside with him, and he walked me around to the side of the car. I promise that in the dark, black and gray practically seemed like the same color. Unfortunately, that was not the case in broad daylight. I had covered the side of my car with what looked like a massive black cloud.

Thankfully I'm much more willing to take responsibility in my life these days. When it comes to all God has in store for your life, I think it's crucial you learn what your part is in it all. When you decide you're going to go after all God has for your life, you'll be tempted with the opposite of not taking enough responsibility. Just as there's something wrong with doing that, you can also get to the place where you take on too much responsibility. Let me give you this big idea, and then I'll let you know how it plays itself out.

In every endeavor, there is a part for you to play and a part for God to play.

God wants you to take responsibility only for your part, and he promises he will take responsibility for his. So often we try to step into the part that's reserved only for him. Or we want him to play the part he's asked us to play. It's important you commit yourself to playing your part but also limit yourself to playing *only* your part. Here are a couple of questions to ask in any situation:

> ## What is the part God is asking you to play? What is the part only God can play?

Starting Epic Church required me to learn this concept I'm now teaching you. It was a massive endeavor, and I needed to be committed to doing everything I could to help the church get off the ground. I knew if I did everything I was supposed to do but God didn't show up and play his part, my efforts alone wouldn't be enough. I could pray, but God would have to answer my prayers. I could try to recruit a team to join me, but God would have to put that calling on their hearts. I could search for facilities in our target neighborhood, but God would have to position things for us to find a helpful landlord with a favorable price. I could invite people to attend our church, but God would need to prompt their hearts to show up.

As I was learning this idea, I wanted it to be the entire foundation our church would be built on. Psalm 127:1 reminds me, "Unless the LORD builds the house, the builders labor in vain. Unless the LORD watches over the city, the guards stand watch in vain." Without a doubt, I know everything we do without God in our church will be done in vain. I'm not that good of a leader by myself. Our musicians aren't talented enough on their own. Our staff is amazing, but not enough if God's power isn't present in their work. I knew we needed God to do what only he could do.

Notice what that verse doesn't say. It doesn't say our part is in vain or it's insignificant. It simply recognizes the reality that our part without God's won't be all that special. But if God is building with us and watching over the work we're responsible for, then anything is possible.

I've spent so much of my life worrying about things I have absolutely no control over. What if nobody shows up at church? What if we don't have the finances to keep our operation going? What if our kids don't get into the schools we think would be best for them? What if no one wants to publish this book? What if a staff member leaves? It's amazing to me how much time and energy we invest in worrying about things we have no control over. I have seen this so often:

We try to control what we have no control over, but we act like we have no control over the things we can control.

I can't make people show up at church, but I can have a say in what the experience will be like when they do show up. I can't control our finances, but I can remember that people give to a compelling vision. I can't force our kids into any school in San Francisco, but I can research, pray, and fill out forms for them. I couldn't force a publisher to want to produce this book, but I could submit a well-written proposal. I can't make any staff member stay on our team, but I can treat them in a way that will make them want to have a future with us.

How do you understand what is your part and what is God's part? While there is no formula for this, I do think there are some ways you can figure out which one of you is supposed to do which part. Praying, being obedient, and trusting are always parts you can play in any process God has you involved in. Usually there will be some action you need to take beyond those. Sometimes, though, everything else will be done by God.

Once again, I'm drawn to the story of Moses, Pharaoh, and a couple million slaves. The people were afraid, and Moses interjected to let them know exactly what their part was and what part God was playing. "Moses answered the people, 'Do not be afraid. Stand firm and you will see the deliverance the LORD will bring you today. The Egyptians you see today you will never see again. The LORD will fight for you; you need only to be still'" (Exod. 14:13–14). Before you take this to be your role in every endeavor, let me tell you being still won't typically be your only role. But let's be honest, if you're anything like me, being still is one of the most difficult parts you'll ever have to play. Is there anything in your life today in which God could be saying, "I will fight for you; you need only to be still"?

When I knew we were going to be starting our church, the thing that scared me more than everything else was the fundraising aspect. But I knew I had to be committed to giving it everything I had. So I did exactly that. I made sure we had a beautiful business plan to show potential donors and church leaders. I got coaching on raising funds. I asked friends to introduce me to their friends in hopes of having their financial support. I drove and flew to meet people, trying to make a case for why they should give to this church we were starting in San Francisco. I followed up with everyone in a systematic way. I was totally working the system, determined to do everything I could to get this church funded.

Then came a week that taught me a crucial lesson I want to teach you now. All of a sudden, it felt like I ran into a wall in my heart and mind. I don't know how to describe it other than saying it became clear to me that I was trying to force my way through the fundraising process. I had been so willing to do whatever it took to raise these funds that I took 100 percent of the ownership for the outcome. When I started feeling this way, I knew I needed to take a step that would somehow show me all of this wasn't on my shoulders alone. I decided to take a one-week break from initiating any fundraising conversations. I would still respond to people who reached out to me with information or questions, but I committed myself to not reaching out to anyone about giving to help start Epic Church.

What happened as a result? I had a peace that had been missing in previous weeks. I had to pray and trust God to move in the hearts of people. Some strong financial commitments came in during that week. We ended up raising over one million dollars to start Epic. I now get asked to teach others about how to raise funds. But I know—and now you know—God was the one who did the heavy lifting in this endeavor.

I like to remind myself that regardless of what my part happens to be, God is always the one doing the major work in my life. And the more impossible the situation seems, the bigger the part God will have to play in whatever I'm seeking to accomplish.

When we were seeking to adopt our daughter, Kavita, Shauna and I were focused on doing everything we could to bring her home as soon as possible. We knew it was expensive. We knew there would be seasons of waiting. It turned out to be a nearly impossible situation. Without knowing all the reasons why, our family was denied adopting Kavita on three separate occasions. We had done our part. We had filled out numerous forms. Thanks to our savings and a great group of friends, we had the financial resources needed to cover her adoption. And yet, we reached a place where there was little more we could do to help bring her home. But we could pray.

Just so we're clear, prayer is never just barely doing something. I remember a specific time in the process when we needed God to move in a major way. We invited friends to come to our house and pray with us. They showed up, and it was a powerful night. We sat out on our back patio, taking turns asking God to intervene in a miraculous way. This was our part to play, even if everyone present wished there was more we could do.

Proverbs 21:1 became a banner verse in my life. "In the LORD's hand the king's heart is a stream of water that he channels toward all who please him." I had to know that whoever was in charge in India, God was in charge of them. I had to believe God really had all authority and he could channel any circumstance in a way that would bring Kavita home to our family.

So how exactly did Kavita get to come home? I'm so glad you asked, because it's a remarkable story. A few things took place that could be described as "only God" possibilities. For starters, a new person stepped into the position overseeing women and children for the entire country of India. The person made it clear that one of her top priorities was to clear the backlog of adoptions throughout the country. Was this merely a coincidence? I don't think so. I think God was doing some heavy lifting—yes, for our specific family, but also for every other family who was praying the same kind of prayers for their own adoption process. And God was making a way for boys and girls throughout India to be put in forever families.

The woman in charge took things a step further. She posted her email address for anyone who needed to get in touch with her. I told Shauna she should go ahead and send an email to her. Shauna asked me, "Should we pray about it first?" I said, "No, we've been praying about it." Essentially, I was saying, "This is now our part." From what we can see in hindsight, this was how God chose to do the heavy lifting in our family and in Kavita's life.

What do you need God to channel in your direction?

One of the best stories that shows our part and God's part is when Jesus feeds thousands of people. The disciples let Jesus know he needs to send the crowds away so they can go to the villages and buy some food.

> Jesus replied, "They do not need to go away. You give them something to eat."
> "We have here only five loaves of bread and two fish," they answered.
> "Bring them here to me," he said. (Matt. 14:16–18)

I'm guessing you know how this story ends, but I want to point out how it perfectly illustrates everything I've been trying to communicate in this chapter. Jesus was asking the disciples to do something they could not do on their own. They did not have enough to feed this entire crowd. Yet there was something they could do. They could bring Jesus what they did have.

Sometimes we feel like we don't have enough, so we don't even put it in God's hands. I think all he expects from us is to bring him what we do have. If what we have isn't enough, then it must not be our responsibility to make up the difference. That is in the category of "heavy lifting," and we must remember it isn't our part.

What are you withholding from God because it doesn't seem significant enough to you? What if he can multiply it, but only if you place what you do have in his hands?

Do everything God asks you to do, and ask him to do everything only he can do.

You are not responsible for everything in the universe or even in your own life. If you constantly feel the pressure of thinking you have to take care of everything and everyone, let that go. What you are responsible for is what you do with your attention, your time, your money, your work, and any area of life where you are the one making the choice. May you find great freedom in letting God take care of everything he alone is responsible for.

NOTES

What is the part God is asking you to play?

What is the part only God can play?

What do you need God to channel in your direction?

What Will Help You?

*There are practices you can implement to
help what is possible become probable.*

15

Redefining Significance

There is a desire in each of us to be special. We long to be valuable and seen as worthy. We want to know that we matter. We want our lives to have purpose and meaning.

If you long to be significant, you don't need to apologize for that. I believe God deposited that longing in you, me, and every other human who has ever lived. Significance means you are worthy of attention. Who doesn't want to be worthy of attention or to be noticed by someone who matters?

Longing for significance, in and of itself, isn't the problem. The problem comes when your longing for significance causes you to pursue it in the wrong way or by chasing after the wrong things.

Where are you trying to find your significance?

Maybe you are seeking significance by trying to please everyone around you. Perhaps you're trying to gain it through your achievements. It could be you're trying to stand out through your physical beauty. Maybe your quest for value is what has led you to pursue multiple degrees from elite universities. Perhaps you have allowed your desire to be noticed to cause you to try becoming the "expert" in your industry. If you're a parent, you may try to gain your significance by living vicariously through your children and their accomplishments. You could seek to find your significance in countless ways: by the number of social media followers you have, by the title you hold at your company, or even by how much you know about the Bible.

Who are you letting determine your significance?

This question is even more important than the "where" question. Are you allowing your boss to determine whether or not you are significant? Are you letting the culture around you decide if you're valuable or not? It could be possible you are giving permission to a company to tell you if you matter enough, simply based on whether they hire you.

We are all tempted to find our significance in the wrong places. I've sought to find mine by being a successful church leader, by giving talks to inspire everyone who is listening, by being seen as a great dad and husband, by being able to solve problems for others, and in so many other ways. I've allowed individuals and groups to determine whether I'm valuable or not. I've let critics, at times, convince me I'm not that significant. I have let my own past keep me from thinking I have worth.

I want to show you a group of people who found their significance in what they could do for God. This is probably the area I struggle with the most, so this story really hits home for me. I think you'll find it compelling as well, since so much of this book is about how you and I can do what God created us to do with our lives.

Jesus sends out a group of seventy-two disciples, in pairs, to go to every town where he was about to go. He tells them

to heal the sick and to preach the good news of the kingdom
of God. They do this, and here is what happens when they
return:

> The seventy-two returned with joy and said, "Lord, even the
> demons submit to us in your name."
>
> He replied, "I saw Satan fall like lightning from heaven. I
> have given you authority to trample on snakes and scorpions
> and to overcome all the power of the enemy; nothing will harm
> you. However, do not rejoice that the spirits submit to you, but
> rejoice that your names are written in heaven." (Luke 10:17–20)

Imagine how excited these disciples were to tell Jesus about
all they had done. Let's be honest, they had done something
very significant. They did exactly what Jesus told them to do.
Maybe they were thinking, *Now we're really significant. He
might have chosen those other twelve guys first, but this is
going to make us stand out to him.* I love how Jesus reframes
their understanding of significance. It's almost as if he is saying,
"That is pretty cool, but let me tell you what matters more than
what you did. The reason you are significant is because your
names are written in heaven. You are known by the God who
created the universe. You are now a citizen of heaven. You have
an identity that is the most valuable one a person could ever
have. You have been called a son or daughter of God." I love
what Pete Scazzero, commenting on this passage, says: "In other
words, he wants them to remember that their joy comes from
their relationship *with* him, not their achievements *for* him."[1]

We want to be thought of as significant. We want someone
important to notice us. We would love to see our names written
down when it comes to awards or recognitions or mentions.
And Jesus doesn't try to talk us out of our quest for significance.
He's simply trying to tell us we've already been given that kind
of significance.

How would things look different in your life if you began to live *from* significance rather than *for* significance?

Whose attention are you trying to get? Because we're all looking for significance, we have to choose which audience we're going to live for. During the longest public teaching he ever gave, known as the Sermon on the Mount, Jesus talks about our desire to be seen (see Matt. 6:1–18). And he speaks about how our reward will be determined by the audience we choose to live for. He warns us not to do what we're doing to be seen by others. If we make others seeing us our aim, we will actually forfeit the reward God has for us. However, he says God sees what we do even when no one else sees it. And when we do it for God rather than everyone else, he will give us a reward.

I don't think Jesus means we should never do anything that will be seen by others. Earlier in this same teaching, he says to "let your light shine before others" (Matt. 5:16). I think he means we need to make sure our reason for doing what we're doing isn't to be seen by others.

One of the most dangerous things for all of us is that other people cannot see what is inside us. Why is this so dangerous? Because all of us are willing to work on the things everyone else can see. Some of us could be spending all our energy trying to convince others we are significant, rather than receiving the truth that God has already made us someone significant.

If you do everything you do to be seen by others, this will be the extent of your reward.

I know you are tempted to live for everyone else's approval. I'm tempted to do the exact same thing. But let me tell you what I have found to be helpful in all this. The only way I can stop doing something isn't to simply concentrate on stopping it. There has to be something else I want more. So here's what I'm aiming at in this area:

I don't want to live for the applause of earth if it causes me to miss the applause of heaven.

Our desire to be seen by God reminds me of the story of Hagar. She is an Egyptian handmaiden to Sarai (later Sarah). When Sarai realizes she can't have children (of course, she's proven wrong by God on this), she gives Hagar to her husband, Abram, so she will give him a child. After Hagar conceives, Sarai isn't happy at all, even though it was her idea. Hagar gets mistreated by Sarai and runs away. An angel sent from God meets her at a time when she must have felt all alone. This encounter is so strong Hagar gives God a title I want to share with you. "She gave this name to the LORD who spoke to her: 'You are the God who sees me,' for she said, 'I have now seen the One who sees me'" (Gen. 16:13).

Have you seen the God who sees you?

God sees you, even when others don't.

God approves of you, even when you don't pass their test.

God focuses his attention on you, even when the world ignores you.

God calls you significant, even when everyone else refers to you as insignificant.

Knowing God sees you can free you from making sure everyone else does.

The only thing stronger than our longing for significance is our fear of insignificance. I've spent so much of my life dealing with this one. This fear can keep me thinking I never do enough. It has caused me to spend way too much time trying to craft an image for myself that I can produce for the world. But more than all that, it has caused me to miss out on the significance God wants to give me.

There's a moment from the end of the life of Jesus that illustrates what happens when we've been freed from finding our significance in the wrong places.

> It was just before the Passover Festival. Jesus knew that the hour had come for him to leave this world and go to the Father. Having loved his own who were in the world, he loved them to the end.
>
> The evening meal was in progress, and the devil had already prompted Judas, the son of Simon Iscariot, to betray Jesus. Jesus knew that the Father had put all things under his power, and that he had come from God and was returning to God; so he got up from the meal, took off his outer clothing, and wrapped a towel around his waist. After that, he poured water into a basin and began to wash his disciples' feet, drying them with the towel that was wrapped around him. (John 13:1–5)

If we knew our time on earth was about to be over and we were going to die a horrific death, we would likely be obsessed with ourselves. Jesus shows us that finding our significance in God keeps us from becoming obsessed with ourselves. He's being betrayed by one of his disciples, and he's going to be abandoned by all of them soon. How could he love them all the way until the end, and what keeps us from being able to love people in our own lives? Jesus loved his disciples deeply, but their opinion of him did not determine whether or not he was significant. We cannot fully love people if we need their approval to gain our significance.

For a moment, I want you to think about Judas and his own quest for significance. He needed what we all need—to know that he was significant. It appears that he sought to be significant by accumulating wealth. He proactively went to the chief priests and asked them, "What are you willing to give me if I deliver him over to you?" (Matt. 26:15). How did he get to this point of selling Jesus out? It wasn't something that happened to him overnight. He made this kind of thing a habit in his life. One time, when a woman poured expensive perfume on the feet of Jesus, Judas objected. Why? "He did not say this because he cared about the poor but because he was a thief; as keeper of the money bag, he used to help himself to what was put into it" (John 12:6). Imagine this for Judas. He was invited to follow the most significant person to ever walk planet earth, and it wasn't significant enough for him.

Getting back to Jesus, I want to draw your attention to how incredible it was for him to wash the feet of his disciples. How could he possibly do this at such a time? Because he knew God had put all things under his power, so he didn't need to have power in the world's eyes. He knew where he had come from and where he was going. In other words, he already knew he had all the significance he could ever need. So he got up from the meal and began to wash the feet of his disciples. What's the big deal, you ask? Washing feet was one of the most *insignificant* things anyone could do. It was reserved for slaves, who were some of the least significant people in this culture. Don't miss this: Jesus was doing one of the most insignificant things imaginable in the eyes of the world. Yet it was one of the most significant things that has ever happened in human history.

Make sure in your own life you aren't calling insignificant what God is calling significant. It doesn't matter where your position or net worth ranks in the eyes of this world. It matters that you do what God has for you to do. But don't forget—your significance comes from the God who sees you.

NOTES

Where are you trying to find your significance?

Who are you letting determine your significance?

How would things look different in your life if you began to live *from* significance rather than *for* significance?

What could you give your life to if you were freed from the fear of insignificance?

16

Don't Outrun Your Soul

I hope what we're learning so far is helping you to be free to give yourself to the work God has called you into for this season of your life. You're becoming the right kind of person. You're doing what you're doing for the right reasons. You're doing it in the right way. You're building your wisdom table and that's helping you so much. You're no longer letting fear paralyze you from moving forward. You're willing to leave some things that are familiar because you don't want to forfeit future opportunities. You're playing your part and you're asking God to play his. You're staying focused and not allowing distractions to take you off course. You're content with what God has given you to do, no longer comparing yourself to everyone around you. You're finding your significance in God's eyes rather than the eyes of the world. You are ready to fully go after it with everything you have.

If this is true for you, I'm so grateful. But your future can still be derailed unless you embrace the following principle:

Do not live an external life that your
internal life cannot keep up with.

The speed of seemingly everything in our world is faster than it has ever been. Through email, social media, and text messages, we can now communicate immediately with other people. Amazon has made it possible to have almost anything we want by the next day. We have multiple transportation options when it comes to getting around town or going across the world. It's no surprise that advancements in technology have increased the speed of so many things. Because of this, we assume everything runs faster and happens more quickly than it ever has.

But there is something that hasn't increased its speed at all, and it never will. What is still operating at the same rate of speed it always has? Your soul. It hasn't gotten any faster. No matter what advancements we continue to make when it comes to technology, your soul will still need the kind of care and attention it always has. As John Eldredge says, "What we assume is a normal lifestyle is absolute insanity to the God-given nature of our heart and soul."[1]

I care deeply whether or not you bring out into the world all that God has put in you. Because I am passionate about you giving your life to your God-given purpose, I want to share with you what might seem counterintuitive. You might think a significant calling means you don't have time for tending to your inner life. I would argue the opposite. Because what God wants you to do in this world is so significant, you cannot neglect tending to your inner world. Jesus said it this way: "A good man brings good things out of the good stored up in his heart, and an evil man brings evil things out of the evil stored up in his heart. For the mouth speaks what the heart is full of" (Luke 6:45).

If what comes out of us is determined by what is in us, then we should give great attention to what is happening inside of us. As Ian Cowley says, "In such demanding contexts, unless we are deeply sustained by the resources which only Christ can give us, we are all too likely to lose our way, and perhaps even our vocation."[2] I don't know about you, but I have seen so many people fall into this reality. If you care about your own vocation, make a commitment now that you will tend to your soul for the rest of your life.

One of the things most driven leaders overlook is their need for rest and replenishment. We tend to wear busyness as a badge of honor, and that has to stop if we are going to be the kind of people God intends for us to be. Mark Buchanan writes,

> A common characteristic of driven people is that, at some point, they forget the purpose. They lose the point. The very reason they began something—embarked on a journey, undertook a project, waged a war, entered a profession, married a girl— erodes under the weight of their striving. Their original inspiration may be noble. But driven too hard, it gets supplanted by greed for more, or dread of setback, or force of habit.[3]

Before you read any further, let me ask you this question:

Is it possible you are in a season where you need to let your soul catch up with the rest of you?

"Fast" and "busy" could be words you feel most comfortable with, but "slow" might be one you need to embrace. This is a challenge for many of us, and it is one of the hardest things for me to do. If you were to ask my family and my coworkers to describe me, not one of them would use the word "slow." They would tell you I'm driven, I have an engine that never seems to stop, and I can't just sit around and do nothing. That's all true. In fact, even when it comes to praying, I prefer to do so while walking. There are many benefits to being wired like I am, but there are also some significant drawbacks. I've been driven to sheer exhaustion more times than I care to admit. Also, when I don't let my soul catch up, it affects how I treat the people

I love the most. Not paying attention to my soul has led to increased anxiety and fear in my life. But even more than that, it has kept me from being able to know and relate to God in a life-giving way.

So how do we take care of our souls? How do we make sure we aren't living an external life that our internal life cannot keep up with? Thankfully, we've been given some great examples.

In Mark 1, we see Jesus healing Peter's mother-in-law during the day and healing people who were sick and demon-possessed after the sun went down that night. This, of course, was part of his mission. It was why he came to earth. Jesus knew his time of public ministry was going to be rather short, lasting right around three years. If I knew what he did, I would have been tempted to never rest. I probably would have thought, *There's too much to do and so little time. I just have to keep going and going.* But that's not what Jesus does. Knowing his mission is so significant and his time is limited, he knows he has to take care of his soul. So after an evening of healing many people and casting out demons, Jesus does this the next day: "Very early in the morning, while it was still dark, Jesus got up, left the house and went off to a solitary place, where he prayed. Simon and his companions went to look for him, and when they found him, they exclaimed: 'Everyone is looking for you!'" (Mark 1:35–37).

Jesus knew he needed something, and he did what it took to get it. He did it while everyone else was still sleeping, at least initially. He left the house, went off to a solitary place, and connected his soul to God through prayer.

Because of the calling on each of our lives, it is vital we learn how to do the same. What rhythms do you have for taking care of your soul?

Jesus spent much of his ministry surrounded by people, both his closest disciples and large crowds. But he wasn't concerned about the fact that everyone was looking for him. Here's a tip you need to learn if you haven't realized it yet: The more impact you make in this world, the more replenishment your soul is going to need.

After his moment in solitude, Jesus gets back to the mission for which he came. We read this in the very next verse: "Jesus replied, 'Let us go somewhere else—to the nearby villages—so I can preach there also. That is why I have come'" (v. 38). Soul care wasn't the only aim for Jesus, but he knew it was necessary to sustain the work he had been called to do. If it was a must for Jesus, do we really think we can constantly produce good work in our lives without taking care of our souls?

Luke tells us something similar Jesus does, but there are two things I want you to notice about his remarks: People wanted Jesus's time, and he often withdrew. "The news about him spread all the more, so that crowds of people came to hear him and to be healed of their sicknesses. But Jesus often withdrew to lonely places and prayed" (Luke 5:15–16). We covered this a little in the chapter on distraction, but we need to learn this lesson: The more you make a difference with your life, the more people will want your time. It's not their fault; it's just naturally the way things work. And of course, you never get more than twenty-four hours in a day, regardless of how many people want your time.

As the crowds are growing around Jesus, it might have been tempting for him to say, "I can't keep withdrawing to connect with God and make sure my soul is restored." I know this temptation well, and I'm guessing you do too. While Mark gives us that one occasion Jesus sought solitude, Luke tells us this was a habit or a rhythm in the life of Jesus. He needed his soul restored. He needed to hear the voice of his Father. And he needed to let his requests be known.

What habits and rhythms do you have to ensure your inner life can keep up with your outer life?

I don't necessarily think we all have to have the exact same rhythms, but I do think we all need to have some practices to help us give attention to our souls. For me, making space in my day to be alone with God has become an anchor for me—especially as my external world has become more demanding through the years. My morning rhythm begins the night before, as I try to get to bed at a reasonable hour. As of this writing, Shauna and I wake up around 5:00 a.m., six days a week. Saturday is the only day we don't set an alarm. I'm not naturally a morning person, but I'm so thankful for this habit that's been formed.

A little over ten years ago, I became convinced if I wanted more time to connect with God, the only option for me was waking up earlier. I'm currently starting my mornings with ten to twenty minutes of silence. I have a mind that never wants to stop, so I try to center myself in God's presence through silence. I spend some time reading the Bible, either working through my plan for the year or focusing on a specific topic that's relevant to what I'm facing that season. I use a journal to record any verses that stand out to me, and I usually write out my prayers as well. Shauna and I spend the last five minutes praying together before we wake up our kids and get ready for the day.

While I've shared what is working for me, don't feel the need to make your rhythms the same. Ian Cowley says this:

> Finding the balance between engagement and disengagement will be different for each of us. Some of us are extroverts who gain our energy from being with people, while others are introverts who need time and space on their own to renew their energy and enthusiasm for being engaged with people and their needs. There must be some disengagement for each of us if we are to have time for prayer, for knowing God and listening to him. In our contemporary culture the overwhelming pressure is to be doing too much, to be overly engaged in doing and not sufficiently invested in being.[4]

Knowing how you are wired and your current stage of life, what rhythms make sense for you to engage in? Choose one, practice it, and pay attention to the results it brings. If it does the soul work you need it to, keep at it. If it doesn't quite hit what you're hoping to experience, try something else.

Now that we've covered the importance of a daily rhythm, let's talk about our weekly rhythms. Thankfully, God has woven this one into his commands for our lives. I'm sure you've at least heard of it, even if you aren't currently practicing it. It's called the Sabbath.

> Thus the heavens and the earth were finished, and all the host of them. And on the seventh day God finished his work that he had done, and he rested on the seventh day from all his work that he had done. So God blessed the seventh day and made it holy, because on it God rested from all his work that he had done in creation. (Gen. 2:1–3 ESV)

I know you're already thinking, *If I could finish all my work in six days, I would probably rest too.* This text is not saying God's work would be finished forever. In fact, God is still at work today. He even works when you and I aren't working. So why does God rest? He doesn't rest for the same reasons we think we should. He isn't exhausted. He's not worn himself out. He's satisfied with the work he's done, and he's enjoying it. Walter Brueggemann says, "God rested on the seventh day. God did not show up to do more. God absented God's self from the office. God did not come and check on creation in anxiety to be sure it was all working."[5]

In this Genesis account of Sabbath, we're called to imitate God, to rest because he rested. But there's an instruction about Sabbath that shows up in Deuteronomy, and it is rooted in something else. This passage might be the one most of us need to hear today.

Observe the Sabbath day by keeping it holy, as the LORD your God has commanded you. Six days you shall labor and do all your work, but the seventh day is a sabbath to the LORD your God. On it you shall not do any work, neither you, nor your son or daughter, nor your male or female servant, nor your ox, your donkey or any of your animals, nor any foreigner residing in your towns, so that your male and female servants may rest, as you do. Remember that you were slaves in Egypt and that the LORD your God brought you out of there with a mighty hand and an outstretched arm. Therefore the LORD your God has commanded you to observe the Sabbath day. (Deut. 5:12–15)

The Israelites had been enslaved in Egypt for four hundred years. God gave them the Sabbath as a way for them to remember what he had done for them and to remind them they were no longer slaves. When they were under Pharaoh's reign, all they did was work. There was not a day off. To Pharaoh, these people were just supposed to be machines that produced their quota for each day. In this system, there was absolutely no rest. So God gave them the Sabbath to remind them they used to be slaves and they did not get their freedom because they worked their way into it. God was the one who had done the heavy lifting to free them. And he wanted them to know that endless productivity wasn't the life he'd called them to live. It isn't the life he is calling us to live either. God gives us this weekly reminder so we can know we aren't here on earth just to constantly produce. Tim Keller says it this way:

> Anyone who overworks is really a slave. Anyone who cannot rest from work is a slave—to a need for success, to a materialistic culture, to exploitative employers, to parental expectations, or to all of the above. These slave masters will abuse you if you are not disciplined in the practice of Sabbath rest. Sabbath is a declaration of freedom.[6]

If you're like me, Sabbath isn't easy to practice. For starters, there is always more to do. I don't know about you, but the to-do list never quite gets done. There are more emails to send, more sermons to write, more meetings to prepare for, more vision to cast, more conflicts to resolve, more house to clean, and on it goes. So if I stop producing for a day, who's going to hold up all the work I'm supposed to be doing? Though this makes practicing the Sabbath a challenge for me, it's also the very reason I need to practice it in some form. I need to be reminded I'm not holding up this world. I am not ultimately responsible for our church. I should practice Sabbath to remind myself who God is and who I am not. As Mark Buchanan says,

> The lie the taskmasters want you to swallow is that you cannot rest until your work's all done, and done better than you're currently doing it. But the truth is, the work's never done, and never done quite right. It's always more than you can finish and less than you had hoped for. So what? Get this straight: The rest of God—the rest God gladly gives so that we might discover that part of God we're missing—is not a reward for finishing. It's not a bonus for work well done. It's sheer gift. It is a stop-work order in the midst of work that's never complete, never polished. Sabbath is not the break we're allotted at the tail end of completing all our tasks and chores, the fulfillment of all our obligations. It's the rest we take smack-dab in the middle of them, without apology, without guilt, and for no better reason than God told us we could.[7]

I love being productive. I love finding ways to maximize my time and energy. Before I leave my office every day, I determine the most important things I need to accomplish the next day. When I get home, I set my clothes out and place my Bible and journal next to my chair so I'm ready in the morning. I use so many of the principles I learned from books like *Deep Work* by Cal Newport and *At Your Best* by Carey Nieuwhof. All this is great. But I often need to remind myself—and now I'm reminding you—we were made for way more than just producing and accomplishing. We were made to know God. And I believe this: Sabbath will not keep us from producing the meaningful stuff God has for our lives. If the God who gave us our purpose is also the God who gave us the Sabbath, then it means we can enjoy this day of no work and still do 100 percent of the work he's called us to do in our lives.

Maybe you think you can't rest in this season. Maybe you're starting a new business or a new church. Maybe you have young children. Or maybe there are just too many opportunities right now that you don't want to miss out on. I know all those are real things you have to work through, but notice this from Exodus 34:21: "Six days you shall labor, but on the seventh day you shall rest; even during the plowing season and harvest you must rest." God is letting us know Sabbath is necessary regardless of what season we are in.

Please hear me—this might not mean you can go twenty-four hours a week without doing any work, but find some adequate space in your week to practice the Sabbath. Have rhythms that will keep your life from outrunning your soul.

NOTES

Is it possible you are in a season where you need to let your soul catch up with the rest of you?

What habits and rhythms do you have to ensure your inner life can keep up with your outer life?

17

Ordinary Life, Extraordinary Moments

I love extraordinary moments. Maybe it's the adrenaline or the dopamine hits, but I enjoy the thrill of having a new idea I think is going to change the world. I also really like the moment when I finally bring something out for the world to experience. How about you? Do you find yourself mostly living for the extraordinary moments?

I want my life to matter, which I often think means it cannot be ordinary or mundane or—God forbid—boring. But what if that's what most of my life and your life is supposed to be? What if all that gets portrayed through social media isn't real life? What if most days are actually intended to be ordinary? What if waking up, enjoying a good cup of coffee, praying, reading a psalm by a lit candle, taking the kids to school, doing good work at the office, having one positive exchange with a neighbor, making dinner for your family or your friends, exercising, expressing gratitude for your day, and falling asleep by

10:00 p.m.—what if this kind of thing is what the majority of our days should look like?

And what if how we live these kinds of normal days has implications for the days that aren't so normal? I don't know about you, but when I read Scripture, it's easy for me to think all our favorite Bible characters experienced extraordinary moments every single day. But that's not at all how it played out. Sometimes the people of God waited centuries to hear God's voice. Moses, who surely had a supernatural life, spent forty years tending sheep. Or think about Jesus. Yes, his last three years on earth had a lot of action, but what about the first thirty years of his life? His first three decades were lived in obscurity. Outside of his birth and his parents leaving him behind at age twelve, we know nothing about this part of his life. Let's imagine how he might have spent these days. I'm guessing he woke up and said morning prayers. He likely went off to do good work, probably building something for someone. I'm guessing he helped his family with dinner duties and then said a prayer before going to sleep. Whatever Jesus was doing during these ordinary days prepared him for all that was to come. And whatever you and I are doing on our ordinary days is preparing us for what's ahead too.

How is your ordinary life preparing you for extraordinary moments?

Formation is constantly happening for every single one of us. You are being formed right now, even as you read this book. Both of us will make decisions today that will lead us to become a certain type of person. As author Robert Mulholland says, "Spiritual formation is not an option! The inescapable conclusion is that life itself is a process of spiritual development. The only choice we have is whether that growth moves us toward wholeness in Christ or toward an increasingly dehumanized and destructive mode of being."[1]

If I asked you to tell me about the life of Daniel, I think I'd know the first few things you would point out. I'm guessing you would recall how he interpreted the dreams of King Nebuchadnezzar and others. You would tell me about how his three friends were thrown into the fire when they refused to worship the golden image the king had set up. And of course, you would tell me about how he survived being thrown into the lions' den. These are extraordinary moments in Daniel's life. But what was he doing on the other days of his life?

I think Daniel's life can teach us so much about how our formation can work and what our normal, daily lives have to do with those moments that aren't so normal. When we're first introduced to Daniel in the Old Testament book that bears his name, things are not good for the Jewish people. In 605 BC, Nebuchadnezzar and the Babylonian army besieged Jerusalem and carried some Jews back to Babylon, where they lived in exile. Daniel was part of this group. The reason he was chosen had to do with his looks, his lineage, and his aptitude for learning. In other words, he was chosen because of his giftedness.

Here's the plan Nebuchadnezzar has for Daniel and the other young Jewish men who are part of this group: They are to learn the language and literature of the Babylonians, they are to have a specific diet of food and wine, and their training is to last for three years. What's the point of this plan? Nebuchadnezzar wants to form these young men, including Daniel, into particular kinds of people. He even goes on to change their Jewish names and bestow on each of them a Babylonian identity.

While you might not be taken into exile to serve under a king, there are people, groups, and forces in our world seeking to form you.

Are you self-aware enough to know how the world around you is seeking to form you?

How is the place you live trying to influence you? Do you recognize how the media is trying to turn you into a certain type of person? What are the chances social media companies are writing algorithms for the kind of person you become? In his book *The Deeply Formed Life*, pastor Rich Villodas writes,

> Whether we know it or not, see it or not, or understand it or not, we are always at risk of being shallowly formed. We are formed by our false selves, our families of origin, the highly manipulated presentations of social media, and the value system of a world that determines worth based on accomplishments, possessions, efficiency, intellectual acumen, and gifts. So we need to be regularly called back to the essence of our lives in God. That essence is one of ongoing transformation; that is, Christ being formed in us.[2]

I am fascinated by the length of time Nebuchadnezzar prescribes for Daniel and these other gifted young men. When you read that the training would take place over three years, what comes to your mind? For me, I can't help but think about how Jesus also trained his disciples for around the same amount of time. There must be something to this math—daily training for just over a thousand straight days.

Formation takes place by what you do repeatedly, not by what you do occasionally.

How does Daniel keep from being formed into the person Nebuchadnezzar envisions him becoming? I think the key is found in Daniel 1:8: "Daniel resolved not to defile himself with the royal food and wine, and he asked the chief official for permission not to defile himself this way." He recognizes what is going to happen to him if he goes along with the plan of those over him. He has to determine he isn't going to be formed by the people or the circumstances around him. I believe everything that happens in his future can point back to this pivotal decision. What Daniel is doing in this moment is making a pre-decision about what he will do and what he will never do.

Do you make pre-decisions before you get to the specific decisions of your life? Have you made a decision about what you will do and won't do with your life, before you face the temptations that are coming for you? Have you decided what you will allow and won't allow when it comes to your dating relationships or your marriage?

If you don't make intentional decisions about your own formation, then you will be formed by everything around you.

Author John Mark Comer says this about our decisions: "We make our decisions, and then our decisions make us. In the beginning we have a choice, but eventually, we have a character."[3] Can you see how your daily decisions are turning you into a kind of person? Think about what you've done with your time and attention over the past seven days. Pretend like you don't know yourself and all you have to go on is the seven-day log of how you've spent your time and what you've given your attention to. It may be impossible, but stay objective if you can. Based on what you have or haven't done in the past 168 hours, try to predict who you might become. Consider how it holds up to Paul's statement in Romans: "Do not conform to the pattern of this world, but be transformed by the renewing of your mind. Then you will be able to test and approve what God's will is—his good, pleasing and perfect will" (12:2).

Not only is there a pattern to this world, but there is a pattern to your life. A pattern is the repeated or regular way in which something happens or is done.

What is the pattern of your life?

Even if you don't know many Bible stories, there's a good chance you're somewhat familiar with the one about Daniel being thrown into the lions' den. I don't want to focus on what happens once he's there, but I do want you to see what takes place before that moment. Darius is now the king, and he, like the previous kings, thinks very highly of Daniel. He plans to set Daniel over the entire kingdom of Babylon. This makes the other leaders jealous, and they look for some way to come against Daniel. At first, they can find no corruption in him. Eventually they realize if they're going to find something wrong with him, it will have something to do with his devotion to his God. They devise a plan and present it to King Darius. They get the king to sign off on an edict: Anyone who prays to any god or human except the king will be thrown into the lions' den.

When Daniel finds out about this new rule, what does he do? "Now when Daniel learned that the decree had been published, he went home to his upstairs room where the windows opened toward Jerusalem. Three times a day he got down on his knees and prayed, giving thanks to his God, just as he had done before" (Dan. 6:10). What part of this verse do you think is most important? It was significant for Daniel to pray with the windows open, facing Jerusalem, but this was not the most significant part. It is important that we pray with a certain frequency, and Daniel prayed three times a day, but this isn't the most important thing we read about him. I believe how we posture our bodies during prayer matters, and Daniel got down on his knees to pray, but this isn't what matters most for him. I believe the last phrase is the most important thing we read about Daniel—"*just as he had done before.*" Daniel had patterns, rhythms, and a way of life that had been formed in him long before he got to this challenging moment. He had already resolved to be a certain kind of person, which led to what he was willing to do and what he was not willing to do. Daniel didn't have a faith-filled moment; he lived a faith-filled life.

How are you currently being formed so that you can make it through whatever is coming for you? What are you doing with your life when no one is watching? What kinds of decisions are you making during your ordinary days? James Clear, the author of *Atomic Habits*, writes, "Few things can have a more powerful impact on your life than improving your daily habits."[4] Imagine a day in the future when you are presented with the most incredible opportunity you could ever dream of. With that picture in mind, what are some daily habits and practices that will get you ready for that moment? If you wait to prepare until the extraordinary moment comes, you will never be ready. Just keep showing up over and over to the things that matter most in your formation.

It is what you do when no one is watching that produces what everyone eventually sees.

Though my whole message in this book is about bringing out all that is within you, most days are about the process. We love performances and we love finishing something so we can show others, but that isn't what happens most days. For the majority of our days, we show up and adhere to a process that hopefully leads to progress. And we wake up the next day and do the same. At some point, all of this leads to the extraordinary moments we've been working toward.

Find deep joy in your daily formation. It matters more than you know, and we will all benefit from the work you're doing when none of us are watching you.

NOTES

How is your ordinary life preparing you for extraordinary moments?

_____

_____

_____

_____

Are you self-aware enough to know how the world around you is seeking to form you?

_____

_____

_____

_____

What is the pattern of your life?

_____

_____

_____

_____

18

Front-End Pain

If we are going to live the life God has called us to live, there is going to be some measure of sacrifice involved. What's your philosophy when it comes to the idea of sacrifice?

There are two ways people tend to think about sacrifice, and I believe they both miss the point. Some people don't think anything will be hard when it comes to stepping into their God-given purpose. They just assume it'll come naturally to them. Or because they've done well at other things, they think they'll automatically be equipped to do something new without it really being a challenge for them. These people underestimate what it's going to take to do the job. However, there are other people who overestimate how sacrifice works. They know something will be difficult in the beginning, which makes them assume it will be challenging forever.

Here's what I have learned about sacrifice and what I want to share with you:

If we will pay the price sacrifice demands on the front end, we will usually experience tremendous blessing on the back end.

It is a natural human instinct to want to avoid pain. All of us have had times when we positioned our lives to stay away from anything that could cause us pain. And sometimes this is the wise thing to do. We should stay away from things that will damage our bodies, our minds, and our relationships. But not all pain is bad. To take that statement a step further, pain is often a sign we're doing exactly what we're supposed to be doing. If we avoid the pain lifting weights gives us, we will never get stronger physically. If we skip out on every difficult conversation with other people, even though it might be painful, we will never be able to work through our conflicts. If we don't experience the pain that comes from waking up in the middle of the night to care for our infants, we can't adequately take care of them.

I use these obvious examples to show how crucial pain is at times to our development and to the outcomes we want most in our lives. Most of us are going to experience pain in life based on what we do or refuse to do. So here's my challenge and encouragement to you:

Choose front-end pain over back-end pain.

Front-end pain looks like taking risks, starting something new, training for an event, and generally doing hard things. Back-end pain is all about regrets, missed opportunities, and wishing we had chosen front-end pain.

When it comes to building community at Epic Church, I've shared this idea with our congregation. We have created a number of groups to foster community for people who attend our church. Our goals for each of these groups are that people find a place to grow in their faith, connect with others, and be cared for. Front-end pain when it comes to finding community includes the following: meeting new people, going to a place you've never been before, and being vulnerable. If I'm honest, all these things make me uncomfortable. I find it much easier to just be with people I already know, go to places that are familiar, and not have to be so vulnerable with strangers. While these things can be painful when it comes to the community aspect, back-end pain is much worse. If you don't go through with the front-end pain, then you pay the price. The costs for this include living in isolation, having no one to care for you, and remaining unknown.

Think about these two versions of pain in your own life. What does front-end pain look like in your situation? What is the potential back-end pain? Let's say you feel like you're supposed to step into a new job opportunity, but it's in a different field than the one you've spent your entire career working in. Front-end pain means you would be stepping into something you don't know how to do yet. It could mean going back to school or teaching yourself how to do something that takes a long time to learn. But what if you aren't willing to sacrifice what it would take? Though you may avoid pain in the beginning, you'll likely live with some pain on the other side. You might feel stuck in the same career you've always been in. Two years from now, you might say, "If I had only started that degree program, I'd already be finished with it and doing the thing I wanted to do in my career."

As you might imagine, when we decided to move to San Francisco to start our church, it demanded quite a bit of sacrifice. We sold the house we were living in, along with most of the possessions in it. I had to walk away from a great job and a stable paycheck. We had to remove our oldest son from a great school he was attending. I had to spend time and energy in raising funds for this new church. We had to move far away from our extended family. These sacrifices were quite costly at the time. Let's assume I didn't want to go through that front-end pain. What if I had just stayed in the good job I had? What if we were still living in that nice house? What if our kids were still in the same school system? Knowing what I know now, I can't even fathom the back-end pain of missing out on all God had for us and thousands of others since we moved to San Francisco.

It absolutely took sacrifice on our part and the part of every other family who moved out to San Francisco to start Epic Church. There's no denying we have all paid a price to be living out here, doing the work we're giving our lives to. We've now been here over ten years. But when someone asks us what it has been like to do this work, you know what word we never use anymore? *Sacrifice*. Why don't we use this word anymore? It isn't because we aren't paying a high price to do this work. It's just that we have experienced so many wonderful things on the other side of our sacrifice.

If you sacrifice for the right thing early on, you will often receive way more than you ever give.

This principle has been so true for us. Because we paid the price to start Epic, we have seen God do so many things that were way beyond what we could have imagined. There are hundreds of people from over fifty nations who show up every Sunday to see what God might have for their lives. I've seen people join our staff who are locked in on the idea that this is what God has called them to do with their lives. We're seeing many people come to faith and come back to their faith. Our closest friends are part of this church community. All four of our kids have served in some capacity in our church, and yes, it was their choice. What do you think that does to my heart?

Because we said yes to San Francisco, Shauna has been able to publish multiple books. Because we moved to San Francisco, God has introduced me to so many wonderful mentors and coaches. I've met people I never thought I would meet. I've traveled to places I never thought I would get to see. I'm writing this book that never would have been written if we hadn't moved out here. Being willing to embrace the front-end pain that comes with starting a church in downtown San Francisco has led us to countless blessings. I'm so passionate about how this works that I want to ask you these questions:

> **Is there any front-end pain you are refusing to step into? If you keep refusing to step into it, what back-end pain will you inevitably be left with?**

Let me now share with you the areas where sacrifice is likely to come.

Time. Whatever God is asking you to step into, it's likely going to require an investment of your time. This sacrifice might mean you cut out television for a season or you say no to some good things you have been saying yes to in your life. Tell yourself, "One day I won't be new at this like I am now, and one day this won't take as much time as it does now." Put the necessary time in now and see how it multiplies later.

Money. There's a really good chance there will be a financial cost to you stepping into something new. There could be new equipment you'll need to buy. There might be monthly subscriptions you should start paying for. There could be a specific conference you should attend or a set of books you'll need to order. It could even be you're changing careers and your initial salary in your new industry will be much lower than what you are used to.

Learning. I referenced some of these things in the previous paragraph, but learning anything new takes hard work. We all like it best when we're well acquainted with something or even seen as an expert. Embrace curiosity and make a commitment to learn all you can about whatever the new thing is. Give yourself grace when that isn't happening as quickly as you wish. Remind yourself if you stick with it now, one day you'll be the man or woman who gets to teach these principles to everyone else.

Comfort. There's an obvious reason we all enjoy things that make us feel comfortable, but that same reason could keep us from embracing what is uncomfortable. It wouldn't be called a sacrifice if you were stepping into something that was comfortable for you. Embrace the discomfort rather than wishing it away. There's no telling what you'll find on the other side of it.

So far, I've sought to be practical with how the idea of sacrifice works. But I also want to remind you the entire Christian faith is built on these principles too.

No one denies the death of Jesus on the cross was a horrific thing. When we read the description about all that happened to him, we can barely even imagine how terrible it must have been. There is no doubt it was the highest price anyone could ever pay. So why go through with it?

Think about this moment in terms of front-end pain versus back-end pain. Knowing it was going to be brutal, Jesus still chose pain on the front end. He could not imagine living with the back-end pain. "For God so loved the world that he gave his one and only Son, that whoever believes in him shall not perish but have eternal life" (John 3:16). If we were ever going to become the sons and daughters of God, Jesus had to choose pain on the front end. I especially love how the writer of Hebrews tells us why Jesus did this: "For the joy set before him he endured the cross, scorning its shame, and sat down at the right hand of the throne of God" (Heb. 12:2). Jesus went through this excruciating pain with great joy. Was it because it didn't really cost him anything? No, not at all. The reason he could embrace great pain with joy was because he knew what it was going to provide on the other side.

None of us will be called to do what Jesus did for us. But whatever God has called you to do, embrace the front-end pain with joy rather than experiencing the back-end pain with much sorrow.

NOTES

Is there any front-end pain you are refusing to step into? If you keep refusing to step into it, what back-end pain will you inevitably be left with?

19

It Will Come Out

Maybe you're still doubting whether you'll ever see what's in you come out of you. Like me, I know you have good intentions for what you want to see produced in your life. Perhaps you already know the person you want to become, you know what you want to accomplish, and you even have hopes for what you want to be known for. But often we don't become who we set out to be, we don't get around to accomplishing what we are meant to, and people don't associate us with what we had hoped. And in these moments, frustration sets in.

When what we hoped would be present in our lives remains absent, we sometimes act like it's all just a mystery. There are certain things we wish were true in our vocations, but for whatever reason, they just haven't happened yet. We want to have intimate relationships with others, but we think we just haven't been lucky in the relational department. We want to have strong character, but we just haven't been able to free ourselves from the negative habits in our lives.

But what if these things don't have to be a mystery? What if there are reasons for what is present in our lives and what is absent? And what if each of us has something to do with what's there and with what's missing?

While we can't control everything, we have much to do with what comes out in our lives.

The Bible gives a name for all the things that are produced in our lives. It's called *fruit*. God intends for our lives to produce specific fruit. Fruit is the finished product. We tend to spend so much time concentrating on fruit in our lives. Promotions. Our weight. The amount of money in our bank account. All of these are fruit, results, outcomes. And fruit is incredibly important. But concentrating on the fruit doesn't make it any better. There is a process involved, and fruit is simply the end result of that process.

For years now, I have been committed to doing the work God has called me to do. And I've also sought to honor God by the work I'm doing. Until recently, I thought it was most important to do work *from God* and *for God*. And I still think those things are really important. As I stated earlier, God has planned specific things for you to do, and you should give yourself to what he created you to do. I also believe we should do whatever we do for the glory of God rather than selfish ambition.

Let me paint a picture for how I used to think about the way this worked. Imagine God handing you your assignment on paper. You leave his presence with that assignment and give yourself fully to it. You give all you have to bring about the best possible outcome. You then bring back the fruit of your work and present it to God as a way to bring glory and honor to him.

But there's one more piece to this I learned. Go back to the image of God handing you your assignment. Only this time, you don't leave his presence to go do the work. You invite him to come and do it with you. This crucial posture was missing for so much of my life. This is what it looks like to do our work *with God*.

Jesus said, "I am the vine; you are the branches. If you remain in me and I in you, you will bear much fruit; apart from me you can do nothing" (John 15:5). When it comes to the fruit you will produce in your life, Jesus made it pretty clear you won't be able to do it on your own. But he even goes a step further. He says you can do *nothing* without him.

God has a vision for what he wants to bring out in and through our lives. But that vision cannot be realized without his help, his presence, and his power. Striving alone isn't going to get the job done. We must remain—or the word I prefer is "abide"—in Jesus. This means we make our home in Jesus and stay connected to him. Our lives cannot produce what God intends for them to produce apart from him. John Ortberg says it like this: "Bearing fruit means that we will do wonderful things in our lives for God and his kingdom, but we don't really have to try all that hard. Instead, we are to make sure that we are 'with God.' That's what it means to 'abide in the vine'—live intimately with Jesus from one moment to the next."[1]

**You cannot bear fruit on your own,
but you are not on your own.**

How do you know the difference between striving and abiding? Striving feels like endless hustle. Abiding involves rhythms of work and rest. Striving tends to bring anxiety. Abiding creates peace. Striving can distract us from what's most important. Abiding helps us to be close to God and others in our lives. Striving is about earning. Abiding is about receiving. Striving leads to despair when there's failure and arrogance when there's success. Abiding keeps us humble yet confident.

Jesus said, "This is to my Father's glory, that you bear much fruit, showing yourselves to be my disciples" (John 15:8). A practice I've been doing lately is simply inviting Jesus into my day. I try to do this as I wake up and when I go to sleep. I invite him into challenging parenting moments with our kids. I invite him into our staff meetings. I want to make a habit of asking him to come into my joy and my pain. I've started asking him to walk up to the stage on Sundays and teach with me. What would it look like for you to do what you do with him?

While Jesus promised us that with him we would bear much fruit, that fruit doesn't usually come overnight. This means waiting will be part of the process when we're seeking to bring out fruit in our lives. It means we will need both patience and perseverance.

One of the most helpful things I've learned over the past decade is the relationship between sowing and reaping. This teaching shows up throughout the Bible, but here is how Paul talks about it in Galatians 6:7–9: "Do not be deceived: God cannot be mocked. A man reaps what he sows. Whoever sows to please their flesh, from the flesh will reap destruction; whoever sows to please the Spirit, from the Spirit will reap eternal life. Let us not become weary in doing good, for at the proper time we will reap a harvest if we do not give up."

All of us will eventually reap what we sow. I use the word "eventually" because there is often distance between what we sow and what we reap, for the good things and the bad. Why would Paul tell us to "not be deceived"? Imagine someone sowing something bad with their life and thinking it will never catch up with them. God is not going to be mocked, meaning we will not be able to escape from what we have sown. On a positive note, this principle tells us we need to hang on in faith, even when we've been sowing a long time and there's no harvest to show for it—yet. Eventually, we will experience the fruit of days, months, or even years of sowing into the right things.

Knowing you are going to eventually reap what you sow, what are some things in your life you need to give up? What habits? What addictions? What behaviors in your dating life? Is there anything you're doing at the office that goes against God's ways? What are you spending too much time on that you should spend less time on? And what are you spending your time on that you shouldn't be spending any time on? Because you *will* reap whatever you sow.

Paul tells us we will reap a harvest if we do not give up. So what are some things you should never give up? Where are you sowing good seed in your life? Where are you being faithful to God's calling?

In his book *Galatians for You*, Tim Keller talks about how new farmers experience anxiety as they watch over the places where they have sown seed. When they don't see anything coming out of the ground, they wonder if it ever will. But in the end, if they've done their part in sowing, the fruit always comes out. Maybe you're new to faith in Jesus and haven't seen the fruit of what you've been doing. Stick with it because he is faithful and he will bring it out. Don't become weary in doing good. Don't give up. But in order not to give up on something, you must have a vision for what it could become.

I wonder how many things I have forfeited because I didn't stick with them long enough. How many times was my breakthrough right around the corner but I bowed out before I saw it with my physical eyes? How about you? Did you get tired of doing what you felt called to do because you hadn't seen the fruit yet?

If you are going to bring out in your life what God put in you, it's going to take patience and perseverance.

I get asked about how we've been able to see what we've seen so far in the short history of Epic Church. I give a number of responses: I believe God's hand has been on our church. I believe we had a great strategy. I think we have an amazing team. Our vision is clear. We had hundreds of people who partnered with us in getting the church off the ground. There are a lot of answers to the question of how we've seen what's happened so far, but guess what isn't an answer? "It happened overnight." I never give that response because it would be a lie. I've also learned this principle in marriage, parenting, work, and physical health.

The most significant things you do in life will never happen overnight.

It is important to learn how to balance patience and urgency. I know it seems like you should have to choose between these two words that bring opposite things to mind. Let me tell you what I mean by saying you can lean into both of them. If you are going to embark on any kind of significant project in life, it's not going to happen in a short amount of time. This is the part where patience is required. So where does urgency come in? Urgency means that, although you realize this project is going to take a long time and require patience, you can do a few things today toward that ultimate goal. And you can wake up tomorrow and take a few more steps. And the next day. And eventually, you're going to arrive at the finish line. As Henri Nouwen says, "Patience means to remain close to the moment and to fully taste where you are so that the seeds that are sown in the moment can grow and lead you to the future."[2]

Don't lose heart. You will reap what you sow. It will come out. Let's assume you're single but you want to be married one day. What if what you're currently sowing as a single woman or man will determine what you reap when you are married someday? What if your position in the company five years from now is determined by what you sow during your current entry-level role? What if what your church community reaps in ten years is based on what you all are sowing right now?

I wish there was a harvest every single day. I wish the harvest came faster and easier than it usually does. But God set things up so there's usually a delay between our sowing and reaping. I think he wants to build faith in us. I believe he wants to grow our prayer life and our dependence upon him. While we can't reap a harvest every single day, we can sow into a future harvest every single day. I can sow into my relationship with God every single day. I can also sow into my marriage with Shauna and my relationship with my kids every single day. I can sow into the future of our church through teaching, praying, and leading.

We cannot reap each day, but we can sow each day.

NOTES

What can you start sowing into today, knowing you will reap a beautiful harvest one day?

Conclusion

Positioned for the Future

I bet you're like me in at least one way. You wish you could know everything about your future. It would be amazing to know where you're going to live, who you will marry, which of your ideas will actually work, and so much more. I get it. We think everything would be so much better if we could only know what our future holds. But I think it would be boring to know the specifics of what's ahead for us. Though uncertainty can make us anxious, I hope it will cause all of us to lean into God and enjoy the adventure. Just because you can't know everything about the future doesn't mean you can't prepare for it. Here's the principle to hold on to in this chapter:

While you cannot know exactly what your future holds, you can position yourself for that future.

Just think about it. Five years ago, you were doing something that positioned you for the life you're living today. You might be thrilled with where you're at in life or you might have several regrets. Regardless, I hope you can see you were somehow positioning yourself for the life you are now living. And it's likely you are doing things in this season that are setting you up for your future.

But how do you position yourself for the future when you're unsure what that future will include? For starters, go back to what you've learned so far. Get a great wisdom table. Fill your soul on a regular basis. Keep building courage in your life. Get out of the comparison game. Pay the price on the front end rather than the back end.

There are a few other things you can do to make sure you're ready for what's coming.

Plant yourself on the right path. The path we choose is going to determine where we end up in the future. To get from my house to Epic Church, I can take several modes of transportation. I can get a ride from Uber or Lyft. I can take the BART train. I can ride my bicycle. I can drive. Not only can I get from my house to downtown using various modes of transportation, but I can also take different roads. You know what I can't do? I cannot take any road I want to and assume I will end up at Epic Church in downtown San Francisco.

When you think about where you want to end up, the same is true. I'm going to assume you have some preferred destinations for your future. What is it that might keep you from ever arriving at your destinations of choice?

Here is a truth to hold on to:

Whatever path you take has inevitable conclusions.

Where is your current path going to take you eventually? Your life is already on a trajectory. If you remain on your current path, there are specific destinations you're going to arrive at. As you look at what's waiting for you, is that where you actually want to go? Through the prophet Jeremiah, God tells us it really matters where we plant ourselves if we're going to arrive at our preferred destinations.

This is what the LORD says:

> Cursed is the one who trusts in man,
>   who draws strength from mere flesh
>   and whose heart turns away from the LORD.
> That person will be like a bush in the wastelands;
>   they will not see prosperity when it comes.
> They will dwell in the parched places of the desert,
>   in a salt land where no one lives.
>
> But blessed is the one who trusts in the LORD,
>   whose confidence is in him.
> They will be like a tree planted by the water
>   that sends out its roots by the stream.
> It does not fear when heat comes;
>   its leaves are always green.
> It has no worries in a year of drought
>   and never fails to bear fruit. (Jer. 17:5–8)

Whether or not you flourish will have everything to do with where you plant yourself.

Look at the differences between these two kinds of people. One trusts in humans, the other trusts in God. The first person depends only on themselves, while the second person places their confidence in God. One of them dwells in parched places of the desert, in a salt land where no one lives. The other is by the water and never fails to bear fruit.

We cannot just plant our lives wherever we want and magically expect we will produce the fruit that God wants to draw out of us. Where we plant our lives is more important than the circumstances of our lives. As you think about your path, is it possible you need to be replanted?

Never stop growing. The best gift you can give yourself and the world is to keep growing for the rest of your life. No matter what you have accomplished or how old you might be, do not live with an arrival mindset. While I don't know what your future is, I do know this—to be ready for it, you must keep developing.

There are two specific areas I want you to focus on when it comes to your growth: *your character* and *your skills*. I love what the last verse in Psalm 78 says as it describes these two areas together: "And David shepherded them with integrity of heart; with skillful hands he led them" (v. 72). I have seen way too many people who are extremely skilled but lack the necessary character. And while character is of vital importance, it's going to take skill for us to step into the unique roles God has chosen for every single one of us.

When it comes to growing your character, concentrate on your *weaknesses*. What are the areas in your character where growth is most needed? What are those things, regardless of what is ahead for you, that will hold you back from being who God wants you to be in the future? Maybe you have a short temper and you know it will be hard to lead in any significant way unless you work on that. It could be you like to gossip and you know that needs to go from your life. Maybe laziness is a current shortcoming you know you'll have to remove from your life so you can step into the thing that will undoubtedly require a lot from you. Here's a question I want to ask regarding your character:

What is present in your life that could hijack God's vision for your future?

Do whatever it takes to grow your character. Ask God to transform the weaknesses in your life. Meditate on Scripture that talks about how to live the right way in these areas. Ask someone in your tribe if they can help you grow your character. See a therapist or a counselor. I've seen too many people who have so much talent that it takes them to a place where their character is unable to sustain them.

When it comes to your skills, focus on your *strengths*. What strengths has God given you? How can you get better at using them? There's a good chance whatever he has for you to do in the future will be aligned with the gifts and talents he has given you.

While I don't know the specifics for my own future, I know it's going to include teaching and leading at a higher level than I'm currently at. It would make no sense for me to give time and energy to developing my gifts as a singer. For starters, I don't possess that gift, and all the coaching in the world probably won't change that. Also, I'm pretty confident God doesn't have anything for me in that area. I can, however, tell you some ways I have grown in my gifts and how I'm trying to do that even now. In 2013, I realized I could be more engaging as a speaker if I could get away from having to look at my notes. I challenged myself to do something I had never done before. I made a commitment to internalize my Sunday messages so well that I would have to rarely, if ever, look at my notes. This meant I would have to spend several hours learning my message by heart. Since that time, I have done this every week before I speak on a Sunday.

Another way to grow your skills is to be an avid reader. Ask the best leaders you know what they're reading. I'm indebted to countless authors who have shaped my own leadership over the past decade. If there's a specific area I'm interested in or know I need to grow in, I read books in that category. If I don't have specific areas, then I tend to read books in the "general leadership" arena. Coaches, conferences, and podcasts have also been invaluable to my growth. As I mentioned earlier in this book, your wisdom table should be a great source of growth for your skills (and your character).

Keep taking steps forward. Often we don't move in a direction unless we already know the final destination. My experience has shown me if we have a general idea of where God is leading us, we don't have to wait until we can see the entire picture. Stop waiting for certainty before you step out and move forward. If you happen to be in a season where you feel stuck, what step could you take? What I have discovered is when we take a step, God tends to illuminate more of our path.

Review your financial health. While I don't know what God has in store for your life, I do know debt or a lack of financial margin could keep you from it. If your finances aren't in great shape, you don't need to feel shame in this area. But you owe it to yourself to get things straightened out. The last thing you want for your life is to be unable to step into an opportunity because of your financial position. What are some financial decisions you can make in this season that will prepare you for a future season, whatever it might involve?

As a leader, I often feel the pressure of knowing all the details about where we're headed. Learning what I've shared with you about positioning has brought me a lot of peace, even when the future seems uncertain. When we decided to start Epic Church, so much was unknown about the future. That being said, there were some things we could do and some decisions we could make to be ready for whatever would come our way.

We learned early on a number of attempted church starts had failed in the Bay Area. As we probed further, we discovered a few reasons why. For starters, some people had tried to start a church all by themselves. A second reason had to do with the sheer cost of living in the Bay Area. We also learned some people weren't willing to put in the work it takes to start a church from the ground up.

After learning these things, we sought to do the opposite. I did everything I could to recruit the best team possible. Our team at Epic has always been one of our greatest sources of strength, even when we don't exactly know what's next for our church. Knowing that the cost of living kept many of those other churches from making it, I set out to raise as much money as possible. By God's grace and the generosity of many churches and individuals, we were able to raise over one million dollars to start Epic Church. We also determined our team would build the kind of culture that valued a strong work ethic.

In 2019, our church began to raise money to purchase our own property. It's common for a church like ours to do that. But here's what isn't common. We didn't have a building yet. We had nothing specific in mind. We simply knew we wanted to position Epic Church for whatever future God had in store. We believed owning our own real estate would be one of the best ways to position our church for the future. But to buy property in perhaps the most expensive city in the United States, we had to start giving to something before we ever knew what it would be, where it would be, when it would be, or how much it would be.

What can you begin doing today that will position you for what's to come? What do you need to learn? What financial decisions do you need to make? What character weaknesses do you need to focus on? If you position yourself in this season, there will come a moment in the future when you will be glad you did.

It is my hope *Bring It Out* helps you create a future you will want to live in. Everything won't be perfect. You will have doubts about whether the plan I've given for bringing out what's been put into you is really going to work. There will be disappointments and setbacks in some seasons. Stay with it during these times. Keep showing up. And remember, God put all of this in you for a reason.

NOTES

What is present in your life that could hijack God's vision for your future?

Acknowledgments

Bring It Out would have never become a reality without the help of so many. I offer my deepest gratitude to you here.

Thank you to my wife, Shauna, who believed I could do this before I did. I love this adventure we share and the assignments we've been given.

Thank you to our four children—Elijah, Sam, Kavita, and Asher. I love seeing each of you bring out all that has been placed inside of you. Keep going!

Thank you, Dad and Mom, for all the love, prayers, and encouragement. I would not have been able to step into the life I'm living if you hadn't overcome so much in your lives.

Thank you to my siblings and their spouses—Lee and Lindsey Pilgreen, Emily and Walter Allen, and Erin and Zach Morrow. I'm inspired by how each of you pursue your purpose, and I'm grateful for how we cheer each other on.

Thank you to Shauna's parents, Harris and Phyllis Malcom. You have always encouraged us to pursue our dreams, even when it took us (and your grandchildren) far away from you.

Thank you to Shauna's sisters, Natalie Malcom and Katie Strickland, as well as Katie's husband, Matthew Strickland.

You have loved our family so well, and you've been incredibly supportive of what we've given our lives to building here in San Francisco.

Thank you to these three couples who pastor Epic Church alongside us—Will and Bea Moraza, Lindsey and Ben Lee, and Seth and Jessica Condrey. Whether we're leading a crowd of people on a Sunday morning or it's just our four families doing the Sunday dinners we started during COVID-19, there is nothing like sharing life with you and giving ourselves to the work that matters so much.

Thank you to the Epic Church community in San Francisco. So much of what I've written about in this book was discovered through what we've learned together. It has been an incredible journey so far, and I still believe the best is in front of us.

Thank you to Steve Stroope, Rick Burge, and Andy Wood. Though I've enjoyed having a number of coaches and mentors, it was the three of you who changed my trajectory as a leader. Thanks for believing in me and what was possible.

Thank you to my Strategic Launch Network family. I love the relationship we share together, and it's such a privilege to reach the cities of North America with all of you.

Thank you to Andrea Doering for believing in this project and how much it could help others. It is a joy to work with someone who is so gifted in their craft. Because you have brought out the gifts placed inside of you, this book has been brought out into the world.

Thank you to Jesus for offering me a life beyond what I ever imagined. Your grace and calling have awakened places inside of me I didn't even know existed. My desire is to honor you with this book and help call others to step into the adventure you have in store for them.

Notes

Chapter 1 *Who* Matters Most

1. Dallas Willard, quoted in John Ortberg, *Soul Keeping: Caring for the Most Important Part of You* (Grand Rapids: Zondervan, 2014), 23.

2. Ken Costa, *Know Your Why: Finding and Fulfilling Your Calling in Life* (Nashville: W Publishing, 2016), 11.

Chapter 2 *Why* and *How* Are Greater Than *What*

1. Cambridge Dictionary, s.v. "ambition," accessed October 18, 2023, https://dictionary.cambridge.org/dictionary/english/ambition?q=ambition+.

2. Ben Pilgreen, "Formation and Ambition with Jon Tyson," April 8, 2022, in *Bring It Out*, podcast, April 8, 2022, podcasts.apple.com/us/podcast/bring-it-out/id1589170794?i=1000556625642.

Chapter 4 Design Alignment

1. David G. Benner, *The Gift of Being Yourself*, expanded ed. (Downers Grove, IL: InterVarsity Press, 2015), 88.

Chapter 5 It's Not Too Late

1. A. W. Tozer, *The Pursuit of God* (Camp Hill, PA: Christian Publications, Inc., 1982), 95.

Chapter 7 Who Belongs?

1. Eugene Peterson, "Introduction to Proverbs," *The Message* (Colorado Springs: NavPress, 2002), 1093.

Chapter 9 Engaging Your Advisers

1. John Mark Comer, *The Ruthless Elimination of Hurry* (Colorado Springs: WaterBrook, 2019), 54.

Chapter 12 Missing What Matters Most

1. J. Oswald Sanders, *Spiritual Leadership: Principles of Excellence for Every Believer*, 4th ed. (Chicago: Moody Publishers, 2007), 94.
2. Sanders, *Spiritual Leadership*, 97.
3. Sanders, *Spiritual Leadership*, 97.

Chapter 15 Redefining Significance

1. Peter Scazzero, *The Emotionally Healthy Leader: How Transforming Your Inner Life Will Deeply Transform Your Church, Team, and the World* (Grand Rapids: Zondervan, 2015), 37.

Chapter 16 Don't Outrun Your Soul

1. John Eldredge, *Get Your Life Back: Everyday Practices for a World Gone Mad* (Nashville: Thomas Nelson, 2020), 7.
2. Ian Cowley, *The Contemplative Minister: Learning to Lead from the Still Centre* (Abingdon, United Kingdom: The Bible Reading Fellowship, 2015), 18.
3. Mark Buchanan, *The Rest of God: Restoring Your Soul by Restoring Sabbath* (Nashville: W Publishing, 2006), 77.
4. Cowley, *The Contemplative Minister*, 42.
5. Walter Brueggemann, *Sabbath as Resistance: Saying No to the Culture of Now* (Louisville: Westminster John Knox Press, 2014), 29.
6. Tim Keller, "Wisdom and Sabbath Rest," Redeemer City to City, July 13, 2021, https://redeemercitytocity.com/articles-stories/wisdom-and-sabbath-rest.
7. Buchanan, *The Rest of God*, 93.

Chapter 17 Ordinary Life, Extraordinary Moments

1. M. Robert Mulholland Jr., *Invitation to a Journey: A Road Map for Spiritual Formation*, expanded ed. (Downers Grove: InterVarsity Press, 2016), 29.
2. Rich Villodas, *The Deeply Formed Life: Five Transformative Values to Root Us in the Way of Jesus* (Colorado Springs: WaterBrook, 2020), xv.
3. John Mark Comer, *Live No Lies: Recognize and Resist the Three Enemies That Sabotage Your Peace* (Colorado Springs: WaterBrook, 2021), 157.
4. James Clear, *Atomic Habits: An Easy & Proven Way to Build Good Habits & Break Bad Ones* (New York: Avery, 2018), 29.

Chapter 19 It Will Come Out

1. John Ortberg, *Soul Keeping: Caring for the Most Important Part of You* (Grand Rapids: Zondervan, 2014), 118.
2. Henri Nouwen, *Following Jesus: Finding Our Way Home in an Age of Anxiety* (New York: Convergent Books, 2019), 124.

Ben Pilgreen is the founding and current lead pastor of Epic Church, a dynamic and diverse church located in downtown San Francisco. Ben loves coaching leaders, whether in church or in business. He is the host of the *Bring It Out* podcast and serves as the Bay Area Regional Leader for the Strategic Launch Network. Ben and his wife, Shauna, have four wonderful children and make their home in San Francisco. Learn more at BenPilgreen.com.

Connect with Ben:

BenPilgreen.com

 @BenPilgreen

 @BenPilgreen